RUSKIN BOND

Animal Stories for Children

B. Jain Publishers (P) Ltd.

D-157, Sector 63, Noida - 201307, U.P

Registered office: 1921/10, Chuna Mandi, Paharganj, New Delhi-110055

Published in arrangement with Rupa Publications India (P) Ltd.

Printed in India

The Regimental Myna

In my grandfather's time, British soldiers stationed in India were very fond of keeping pets, and there were few barrack-rooms where pets were not to be found. Dogs and cats were the most common, but birds were also great favourites.

In one instance, a bird was not only the pet of a barrack-room but of a whole regiment. His owner was my grandfather, Private Bond, a soldier of the line who had come out to India with the King's Own Scottish Rifles.

The bird was a myna, common enough in India, and Grandfather named it Dickens after his favourite author. Dickens came into Grandfather's possession when quite young, and he was soon a favourite with all the men in the barracks at Meerut, where the regiment was stationed. Meerut was hot and dusty; the curries were hot and spicy; the General in command was hot-tempered and crusty.

Keeping a pet was almost the sole recreation for the men in barracks. Because he was tamed so young, Dickens (or Dicky for short) never learned to pick up food for himself.

Instead, just like a baby bird, he took his meals from Grandfather's mouth. And other men used to feed him in the same way. When Dickens was hungry, he asked for food by sitting on Grandfather's shoulders, flapping his wings rapidly, and opening his beak.

Dicky was never caged, and as soon as he was able to fly he attended all parades, watched the rations being issued, and was present on every occasion which brought the soldiers out of their barracks. When out in the country, he would follow the regiment or party, flying from shoulder to shoulder, or from tree to tree, always keeping a sharp look-out for his enemies, the hawks. Sometimes he would choose a mounted officer as a companion; but after the manoeuvres were over he would return to Grandfather's shoulder.

One day there was to be a General's inspection, and the Colonel gave orders that Dicky was to be confined, so that he wouldn't appear on parade.

'Lock him away somewhere, Bond,' the Colonel snapped. 'We can't have him flapping all over the parade-ground.'

Dickens was put into a storeroom, with the windows closed and the door locked. But while the General's inspection was going on, the mess orderly, who wanted something from the storeroom and knew where to find the key, opened the door.

PANTRY

Out flew Dickens. He made straight for the parade-ground, greatly excited at being let out and chattering loudly.

Dicky must have thought the General had something to do with his detention, or else he may have felt an explanation was due to him. Whatever his reasoning, he chose to alight on the General's pith helmet, between the plumes.

Here he chattered faster than ever, much to the surprise of the General, who was obliged to take his helmet off before he could dislodge the bird. 'What the Dickens!' exclaimed the General, going purple in the face—for Dicky had discharged his breakfast between the plumes of the helmet. Meanwhile, Dicky had flown to the Colonel's shoulder to make further complaints, to the great delight of the men.

'Fall out, Bond!' the Colonel screamed. 'Take this bird away—for good! I don't want to see it again!'

A crestfallen Private Bond returned to the barracks with Dicky, wondering what to do next. To part with Dicky, or even to cage him, was out of the question.

But Grandfather was not the only one who loved Dickens. He was also extremely popular with the entire battalion. In the end, Grandfather decided to ask his Captain to bring him before the Colonel so he could ask forgiveness for Dicky's behaviour.

The Colonel gave Private Bond and his Captain a patient hearing. Then the Colonel consulted his officers and decided that the bird could stay—provided he was taken on as a serving member of the regiment!

Dickens' popularity was not surprising, as he was highly intelligent. He knew the men of his own regiment from those of others, and would only associate with the Scottish Rifles. Even in the drill season, when there were as many as twenty regiments in camp, Dicky never made a mistake.

Dickens had a unique method of getting from one part of the camp to another.

Instead of flying over the top of the camp, he would go in stages from tent to tent, flying very low, sheltering in each one, then peeping out and looking carefully for hawks before moving on to the next.

One day, Grandfather was admitted to hospital with malaria. Dicky couldn't find him anywhere, and searched and searched all over the camp in great distress. The hospital was a couple of kilometres away from the barracks, and it wasn't until the third day of searching that Dickens finally discovered Grandfather lying there.

From then on, for as long as Grandfather was on the sick list, Dicky spent his time at the hospital. An upturned helmet was placed on a shelf for him near Grandfather's bed, and Dickens spent the night inside it. As soon as Grandfather was discharged from the hospital, Dickens left as well, and never returned, not even for a visit.

In 1888, the regiment got orders to proceed to Calcutta, en route for Burma, where it was to take part in the Chin Lushai Expedition. All pets had to be left behind, and Dickens was no exception.

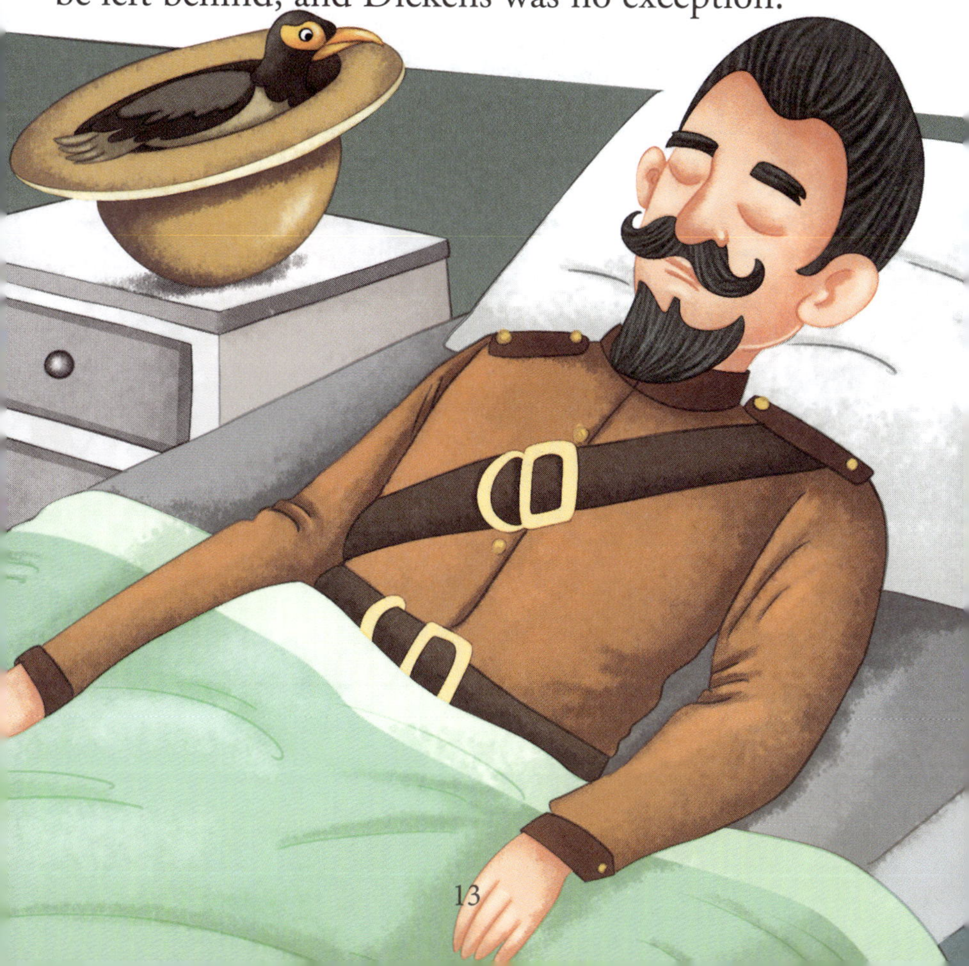

But Dicky had his own views on the subject.

The regiment travelled in stages, marching along the Grand Trunk Road, moving at night and going into rest camps for the day.

Dickens caught up on the third day. He arrived in camp after a journey of more than three hundred kilometres—dull, dejected and starving, as he still depended on being fed from Grandfather's mouth. Route-marching and travelling by train (the railway was just beginning to spread across India), the battalion finally reached Calcutta. From

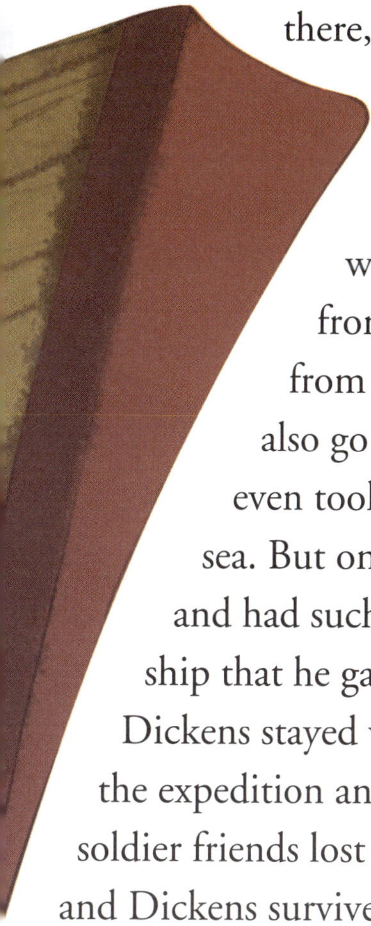

there, contrary to orders, Dickens embarked for Burma along with the soldiers.

On board the ship, Dickens would amuse himself by peeping from the portholes, and flapping from one to the other. He would also go up on deck, and sometimes even took experimental flights out to sea. But one day he was caught in a gale and had such difficulty getting back to the ship that he gave up that kind of adventuring. Dickens stayed with his regiment all through the expedition and the campaign. Many of his soldier friends lost their lives, but Grandfather and Dickens survived the fighting and returned safely to Calcutta.

Grandfather, now a Corporal, was given six months' home leave, along with the rest of the regiment. This meant sailing home to England.

During the first part of the voyage, Dicky was his usual cheerful self. But when the ship left the Suez Canal, the weather grew cold, and he was no longer to be seen on the yardarms or on the bridge with the captain. He even lost interest in going on deck with Grandfather, preferring to stay with the parrots on the waste deck.

After the ship passed Gibraltar, Dickens went below. He never came on deck again. Dickens was laid out in a Huntley and Palmer's biscuit tin, and buried at sea.

Not, perhaps, with full military honours, but certainly to the sound of Grandfather's bagpipes, playing The Last Post.

Tiger My Friend

On the left bank of the river Ganges is a long stretch of heavy forest. There are villages on the fringe of the forest, inhabited by farmers and herdsmen. Big-game hunters came to the area for many years, and as a result the animals had been getting fewer. The trees, too, had been disappearing slowly; and as the animals lost their food and shelter, they moved further into the Himalayan foothills.

There was a time when this forest had provided a home for some forty tigers, but now there remained only one old tiger in the jungle. The hunters had tried to get him, too, but so far he had survived all attempts on his life.

Although the tiger had passed the prime of his life, he had lost none of his majesty. He walked through the long grass with the confidence of one who knew that he was still a king, although his subjects were fewer.

The tiger was heading for a large marsh, where he sometimes went to drink or cool off.

The tiger waited in the shelter of a rock, his ears pricked for any unfamiliar sound. He knew that it was here that hunters sometimes waited for him with guns.

He walked into the water and drank slowly. He raised his head and listened, one paw suspended in the air.

A strange sound had come to him on the breeze, and he was wary of strange sounds. So he moved swiftly into the shelter of the tall grass that bordered the marsh, and climbed a hillock until he reached his favourite rock that was big enough to hide him.

The sound he had heard was only a flute. It belonged to Nandu, a slim brown boy who rode a buffalo. Chottu, a slightly smaller boy, riding another buffalo, brought up the rear of the herd. The herd belonged to the families of Nandu and Chottu. Their fathers sold buffalo-milk and butter in villages further down the river.

The tiger had often seen them at the marsh, and he was not bothered by their presence. He knew the village folk would leave him alone as long as he did not attack their buffaloes. And as long as there were deer in the jungle, he would not be interested in other prey.

He decided to move on and find a cool shady place in the heart of the jungle, where he could rest during the hot. At night he would hunt. With a lazy grunt that was half a roar, 'A-oonh!'—he got off his haunches and sauntered off into the jungle.

The boys, who were barely fifty yards distant, looked up immediately.

'There he goes!' said Nandu, pointing towards the hillock.

'He's a big tiger!'

'Don't' call him tiger. Call him Uncle. It's unlucky to call a tiger a tiger. But if you call him Uncle, he will leave you alone.'

'I see,' said Chottu. 'You have to make him a relative. I'll try and remember that.'

It was evening when the buffalo herd finally made its way homeward.

When Nandu and Chottu came home they found a crowd of curious villagers surrounding a jeep in which sat three strangers with guns. They were hunters.

They had heard that there was a tiger in the area, and they wanted to shoot it. As most of the villagers were poor, they were prepared to go into the forest to make a machaan or tree-platform for the hunters. Nandu was told by his father to tie a goat at the foot of the tree. While these preparations were being made, Chottu had no wish to see the tiger killed. So he tied up bits and pieces of old clothing on small trees and bushes. He knew the wily old king of the jungle would keep well away from the area if he saw the bits of clothing – for where there were men's clothes, there would be men.

The vigil kept by the hunters lasted all through the night, but the tiger did not come near the tree. Perhaps he'd got Chottu's warning; or perhaps he wasn't hungry.

The hunters looked grumpy as they trudged back to the village and drove away.

It was not until the beginning of the summer that something happened to alter the hunting habits of the tiger and bring him into conflict with the villagers.

There had been no rain for almost two months, and the tall jungle grass had become dry and yellow. Some city-dwellers, camping near the forest, had been careless and had started a forest fire. The acrid fumes smoked the tiger out towards the edge of the jungle. As night came on, the tiger turned and made for the marsh, where he knew he would be safe provided he swam across to the little island in the centre.

Next morning he was on the island, which was untouched by the fire. But his surroundings had changed. The slopes of the hills were black with burnt grass, and most of the tall bamboo had disappeared. The deer and the wild pig moved further east.

When the fire had died down and the smoke had cleared, the tiger prowled through the forest again but found no game.

Even now he hesitated to leave the area in search of new hunting grounds, for he had a deep fear and suspicion of the unknown forests further east—forests that were fast being swept away by human habitation. He could have gone into the high mountains, but they did not provide him with the long grass he needed for cover.

At break of day he came to the marsh. He drank, and then lay down across his favourite rock, hoping for a deer; but none came. He was about to get up and lope away when he heard an animal approach. The tiger at once flattened himself on the ground, his tawny stripes merging with the dry grass.

A buffalo emerged from the jungle and came to the water. The buffalo was alone. He moved leisurely towards the water, completely unaware of the tiger's presence.

The tiger hesitated before making his charge.

It was many years since he had killed a buffalo, and he knew instinctively that the villagers would be angry. But the pangs of hunger overcame his caution. He moved in for the kill.

Although he had been starving for days, he could not finish the huge carcass. He dragged the remains of the buffalo into the bushes, to conceal it from jackals and vultures; then he went off to find a place to sleep.

He would return to the kill when he was hungry.

Next day, when Nandu and Chottu came running home to say that they had found the half-eaten carcass near the marsh, the men of the village grew angry. They knew that once the tiger realised how easy it was to kill their animals, he would make a habit of doing so.

Kundan Singh, Nandu's father, who owned the buffalo, said he would go after the tiger himself. Accompanied by Chottu's father and several others, Kundan set out for the marsh. They made another tree-platform in a tall tree some thirty feet from the kill.

Kundan Singh and Chottu's father settled down for the night on their platform.

Just as the moon came up over the hills, the two men were startled by a low rumbling growl.

A moment later the tiger walked out into the moonlight and stood over his kill.

At first Kundan could do nothing. He was completely taken aback by the size of the tiger. Chottu's father had to nudge him, and then Kundan quickly put the gun to his shoulder, aimed at the tiger's head, and pressed the trigger.

The gun went off with a flash and two loud bangs.

The tiger roared and bounded off into the forest.

'You missed him completely,' said Chottu's father.

'I did not,' said Kundan. 'You heard him roar! Would he have been so angry if he had not been hit?'

‘Well, if you have only wounded him, he will turn into a man-eater—and where will that leave us?’

‘He won’t be back,’ said Kundan. ‘He will leave this area.’

During the next few days the tiger lay low. The herdsmen and villagers decided that the tiger had gone away. Nandu and Chottu began bringing the buffaloes to the marsh again during the day.

But one day, while the boys were taking the herd home, one of the buffaloes lagged behind. Nandu heard an agonised bellow behind him. He glanced over his shoulder just in time to see the tiger dragging the buffalo into a clump of bamboo.

Together, the boys and the buffaloes stampeded out of the forest.

'The tiger!' called Nandu. 'He is back! He has taken another buffalo!'

'He is afraid of us no longer,' thought Chottu. 'And now everyone will hate him and do their best to kill him.'

'I will take my gun and a few men, and wait near the bridge. The rest of you must beat the jungle from this side and drive the tiger towards me. He will not escape this time!' said Kundan.

The tiger was still eating when he heard the men coming. With an angry 'Whoof!' he bounded into the jungle.

The tiger hated and feared the noise made by humans.

He was not a man-eater and he would not attack a man unless he was very angry or very frightened; and as yet he was neither.

Chottu felt sorry for the tiger.

'Do they have to kill the tiger?' he asked. 'If they drive him across the river he won't come back, will he?' 'Who knows?' said Nandu. 'He has found it's easy to kill our buffaloes, and when he's hungry he'll come again. We have to live too.'

Chottu was silent. He could see no way out for the tiger.

It was about noon when the tiger finally came into the open. The beaters had done their work well.

The tiger was now only about a-hundred-and-fifty yards from the place where Kundan Singh waited.

Kundan Singh fired and missed.

The tiger rushed forward, making straight for the suspension bridge.

Kundan fired again.

The tiger bounded forward, lost his footing on the slippery planks of the swaying bridge, and went over the side, falling into the river. The current took him away, and before long he was lost to view.

At first the villagers were glad—they felt their buffaloes were safe. Then they began to feel that something had gone out of their lives, out of the life of the forest. The forest had been shrinking year by year, as more people had moved into the area; but as long as the tiger had been there and they had heard him roar at night, they had known there was still some distance between them and the ever-spreading towns and cities. Now that the tiger had gone, it was as though a protector had gone.

The boys lay flat on their little mud island.

'The king of the jungle is dead,' said Nandu. 'There are no more tigers.'

'There have to be tigers,' said Chottu. 'Can there be an India without tigers?'

The river had carried the tiger many miles away from his old home and brought him ashore on the opposite bank of the river.

He saw trees and tall grass. Slowly he heaved himself off the ground and moved to the tall grass. There was no smell of man.

The tiger moved forward with greater confidence. There was, however, another smell in the air—the smell of a tigress.

He gave a deep roar, 'A-oonh!' And the roar came back to him; a roar that meant there would be more tigers in the land!

That night, half asleep on his cot, Chottu heard the tigers roaring to each other across the river, and he recognised the roar of his own tiger. He knew that it was alive and safe; and he was glad.

'Let there be tigers forever,' he whispered before he fell asleep.

Monkey Trouble

Grandfather bought Tutu from a street entertainer. Grandmother at first objected to having a monkey in the house. 'You have enough pets as it is,' she said, referring to Grandfather's goat, several white mice, and a small tortoise.

'But I don't have any,' I said.

'You're wicked enough for two monkeys. One boy in the house is all I can take.'

‘Ah,’ said Grandfather triumphantly. ‘This is a little girl monkey!’ Grandmother gave in. She believed girls were less troublesome than boys. Tutu was to prove her wrong.

She was a pretty little monkey. Her bright eyes sparkled with mischief. And her teeth, which were a pearly white, were often revealed in a grin that frightened the wits out of Aunt Ruby, whose nerves had already suffered from the presence of Grandfather’s pet python. But this was my grandparents’ house, and aunts and uncles had to put up with our pets.

One of the first things I taught Tutu was to shake hands, and this she insisted on doing with all who visited the house. Peppery Major Malik would have to stoop and shake hands with Tutu before he could enter the drawing room, otherwise Tutu would climb onto his shoulder and stay there, roughing up his hair and playing with his moustache.

Uncle Benji couldn't stand any of our pets and took a particular dislike to Tutu, who was always making faces at him. But as Uncle Benji was never in a job for long, and depended on Grandfather's good-natured generosity, he had to shake hands with Tutu, like everyone else.

On one of Aunt Ruby's visits, loud shrieks from her bedroom brought us running to see what was wrong. It was only Tutu trying on Aunt Ruby's petticoats! They were much too large and when Aunt Ruby entered the room, all she saw was a faceless white blob jumping up and down on the bed.

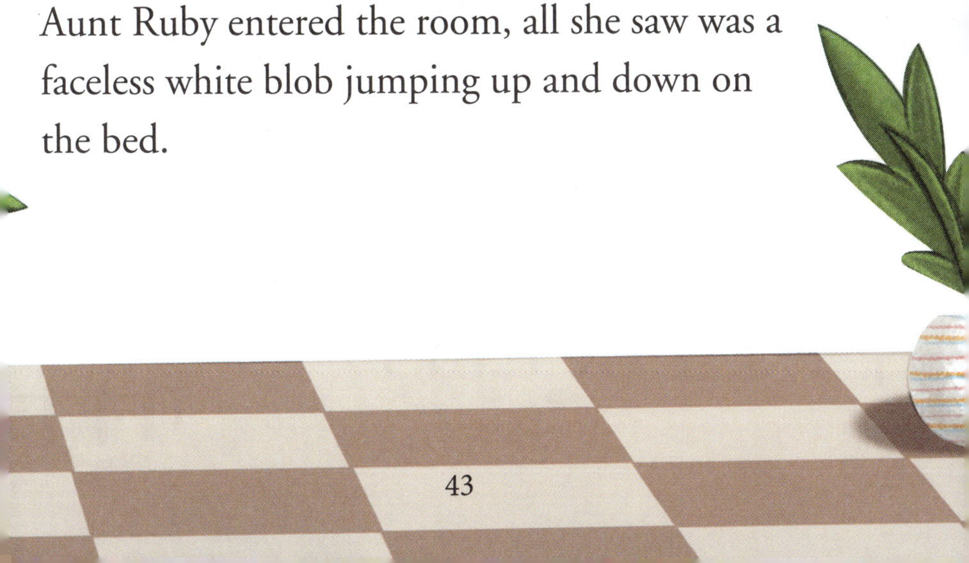

We disentangled Tutu and soothed Aunt Ruby. Then Uncle Benji complained that his hairbrush was missing. We found Tutu using the hairbrush to scratch her armpits.

I took it from her and handed it back to Uncle Benji with an apology; but he flung the brush away with an oath. 'Tutu doesn't have fleas!' I said.

'No, and she bathes more often than Benji,' said Grandfather. All the same, Grandmother objected to Tutu being given the run of the house. Tutu had to spend her nights in the outhouse, in the company of the goat. It was not long before Tutu was seen

sitting comfortably on the back of the goat, while the goat roamed the garden.

The day Grandfather had to visit Meerut to collect his railway pension, he decided to take Tutu and me along to keep us both out of mischief, he said. To prevent Tutu from wandering about on the train, she was provided with a large black travelling bag. This, with some straw at the bottom, became her compartment. Grandfather and I paid for our seats, and we took Tutu along as hand baggage.

There was enough space for Tutu to look out of the bag occasionally, and to be fed with bananas and biscuits, but she could not get her hands through the opening and the canvas was too strong for her to bite her way through.

Tutu's efforts to get out only had the effect of making the bag roll about on the floor or occasionally jump into the air—an exhibition that attracted a curious crowd of onlookers at the Dehra and Meerut railway stations.

While Grandfather was producing our tickets at the turnstile, Tutu suddenly poked her head out of the bag and gave the ticket collector a wide grin.

The poor man was taken aback. But, with a great presence of mind, he said, 'Sir, you have a dog with you. You'll have to buy a ticket for it.'

'It's not a dog!' said Grandfather indignantly.

'This is a baby monkey, closely related to the human species! And there is no charge for babies!'

'It's as big as a cat,' said the ticket collector. 'Cats and dogs have to be paid for.' Five rupees were handed over as Tutu's fare.

Winters in North India can be very cold. A great treat for Tutu on winter evenings was the large bowl of hot water given to her by Grandfather for a bath. Tutu would cunningly test the temperature with her hand, then gradually step into the bath until she was in the water upto her neck.

She would take the soap in her hands or feet and rub herself all over. When the water became cold, she would get out and run as quickly as she could to the kitchen fire in order to dry herself.

One day, Tutu almost succeeded in boiling herself alive. Grandmother had left a large kettle on the fire for tea. Finding the water just warm enough for a bath, Tutu got in. This was fine for a while, until the water began to get heated. Tutu raised herself a little. But finding it cold outside, she sat down again. She continued hopping up and down for some time, until Grandmother returned and hauled her, half-boiled, out of the kettle.

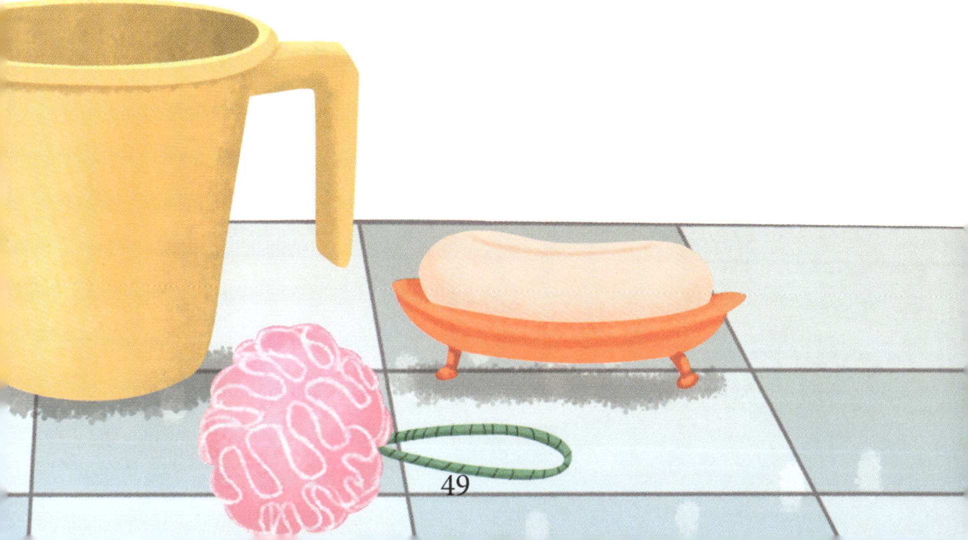

'What's for tea today?' asked Uncle Benji gleefully. 'Boiled eggs and a half-boiled monkey?'

One day Aunt Ruby took us all by surprise. She announced that she had become engaged to Rocky Fernandes, a school teacher from Goa.

Rocky visited the house quite often and brought me chocolates and cashew nuts, of which he seemed to have an unlimited supply. Naturally, I approved of Rocky.

One day, I overheard them talking of going to the bazaar to buy an engagement ring. I decided I would go along, too. But as Aunt Ruby had made it clear that she did not want me around, I decided that I had better follow at a discreet distance. Tutu decided to follow me. But as I had not invited her along, she too decided to keep out of sight.

I waited until Aunt Ruby and Rocky had settled down in a large jewellery shop before sauntering past and spotting them, as though by accident. Aunt Ruby wasn't too pleased at seeing me, but Rocky waved and called out, 'Come and join us!'

While the jeweller and Aunt Ruby were sifting through the diamond rings, Tutu had slipped into the shop without being noticed by anyone but me. A little squeal of delight was the first sign she gave of her presence. Everyone looked up to see her trying on a pretty necklace.

'And what are those stones?' I asked.

'They are pearls,' said the shopkeeper, making a grab for them.

'It's that dreadful monkey!' cried Aunt Ruby. The necklace was already adorning Tutu's neck. I thought she looked rather nice in pearls, but she gave us no time to admire the effect. Tutu made for the crowded road. I ran after her, shouting out to her to stop, but she wasn't listening.

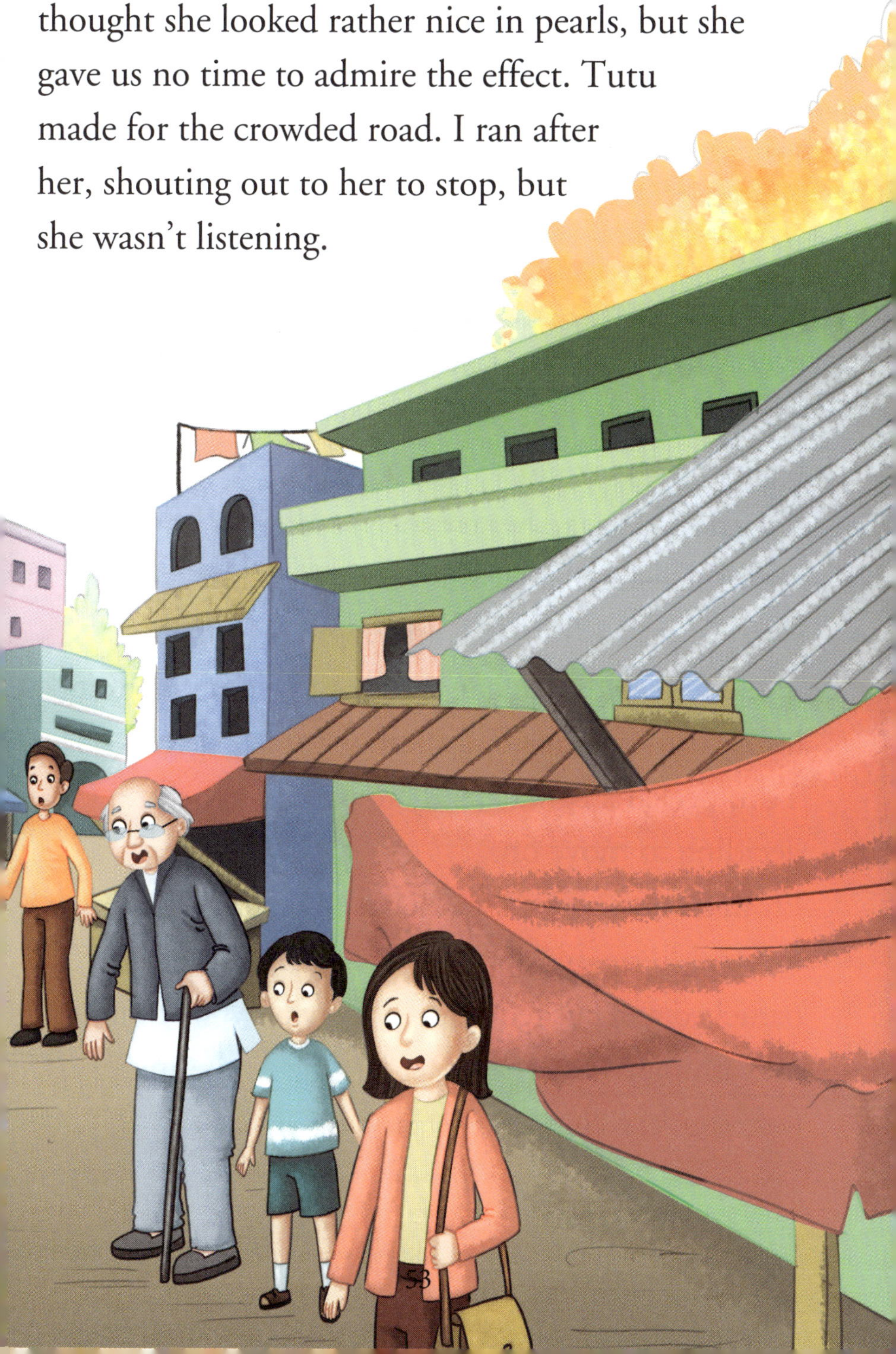

Tutu used the heads and shoulders of people as springboards and so made rapid headway through the bazaar.

The jeweller left his shop and ran after us. So did Rocky. So did several bystanders who had seen the incident. And others, who had no idea what it was all about, joined in the chase. As Grandfather used to say, 'In a crowd, everyone plays follow-the-leader, even when they don't know who's leading.' Not everyone knew that the leader was Tutu. Only the front runners could see her.

She tried to make her escape speedier by leaping onto the back of a passing scooterist. The scooter swerved into a fruit stall and came to a standstill under a heap of bananas, while the scooterist found himself in the arms of an indignant fruitseller.

Tutu peeled a banana and ate part of it, before deciding to move on.

From an awning, she made an emergency landing on a washerman's donkey. The donkey promptly panicked and rushed down the road, while bundles of washing fell by the wayside. The washerman joined in the chase.

Tutu finally decided to end the chase by ridding herself of the necklace. Removing it from her neck, she flung it in the small canal that ran down the road.

The jeweller plunged into the canal. So did Rocky. So did I. So did several other people, both adults and children. It was to be a treasure hunt!

Some twenty minutes later, Rocky shouted, 'I've found it!' He presented the necklace to the relieved shopkeeper.

Everyone trudged back to the bazaar. Aunt Ruby was still in the shop.

Finally the ring was bought and a date was set for the wedding.

'I don't want that monkey anywhere near us on our wedding day,' declared Aunt Ruby.

A few days before the wedding I found Tutu in the kitchen, helping Grandmother prepare the wedding cake.

Tutu often helped with the cooking and, when Grandmother wasn't

looking, added herbs, spices, and other interesting items to the pots—so that occasionally we found a chilli in the custard or a strawberry floating in the chicken soup.

Sometimes these additions improved a dish, sometimes they did not. Uncle Benji lost a tooth when he bit firmly into a sandwich which contained walnut shells.

I'm not sure exactly what went into that wedding cake when Grandmother wasn't looking but I did spot Tutu stirring in some red chilli sauce, bitter gourd seeds, and a generous helping of egg shells!

The great day dawned, and the wedding guests made their way to the little church.

I had offered to dress Tutu up as a bridesmaid but no one except Grandfather thought it was a good idea. So I was an obedient boy and locked Tutu in the outhouse. I did, however, leave the skylight open a little.

The wedding ceremony went without a hitch.

When the service was over, we made our way back to the house for the reception.

The feast had been laid out on tables in the garden.

Tutu was on her best behaviour.

She had, it appeared, used the skylight and now sat beside the three-tier wedding cake, guarding it against crows, squirrels and the goat. She greeted the guests with squeals of delight.

It was too much for Aunt Ruby. She flew at Tutu in a rage. And Tutu, sensing that she was not welcome, leapt away, taking with her the top tier of the wedding cake.

We followed her into the orchard, only to find that she had climbed to the top of the jackfruit tree. From there she proceeded to pelt us with bits of wedding cake. She had also managed to get hold of a bag of confetti, and when she ran out of cake she showered us with confetti.

'That's more like it!' said the good-humoured Rocky. 'Now let's return to the party, folks!'

When the festivities were finally over, Uncle Benji took the old car out of the garage. He was going to drive Aunt Ruby and Rocky to the nearby hill resort of Mussoorie, where they would have their honeymoon.

Aunt Ruby climbed into the back seat. She waved regally to everyone. Everyone wished them luck. The car shot forward in a cloud of dust.
Rocky and Aunt Ruby continued to wave at us. And so did Tutu, from her perch on the rear bumper!

She was clutching a bag in her hands and showering confetti on all who stood in the driveway.

'They don't know Tutu's with them!' I exclaimed. 'She'll go all the way to Mussoorie!'

'Tutu might ruin the honeymoon,' said Grandfather. 'But don't worry—our Benji will bring her back!'

Goodbye, Miss Mackenzie

The Oaks, Holly Mount, The Parsonage, The Pines, Dumbarnie, Mackinnon's Hall, and Windermere. These are names of some of the old houses that still stand on the outskirts of one of the larger Indian hill-stations. They were built over a hundred years ago by British settlers who sought relief from the searing heat of the plains. A few fell into decay and are now inhabited by wild cats, owls, goats, and the occasional mule-driver. Others survive.

Among these old mansions stands a neat, white-washed cottage, Mulberry Lodge. And in it lived an elderly British spinster named Miss Mackenzie. She was sprightly and wore old-fashioned but well-preserved dresses. Once a week, she walked up to town and bought butter, jam, soap and sometimes a bottle of eau-de-cologne.

Miss Mackenzie had lived there since her teens, before World War I. Her parents, brother, and sister were all dead.

She had no relatives in India, and lived on a small pension and gift parcels sent by a childhood friend. She had few visitors – the local padre, the postman, the milkman. Like other lonely old people, she kept a pet, a large black cat with bright, yellow eyes. In a small garden, she grew dahlias, chrysanthemums, gladioli and a few rare orchids. She knew a great deal about wild flowers, trees, birds, and insects. She never seriously studied them, but had an intimacy with all that grew and flourished around her.

It was September, and the rains were nearly over. Miss Mackenzie's African marigolds were blooming. She hoped the coming winter wouldn't be too severe because she found it increasingly difficult to bear the cold. One day, as she was puttering about in her garden, she saw a schoolboy plucking wild flowers on the slope above the cottage. 'What are you up to, young man?' she called.

Alarmed, the boy tried to dash up the hillside, but slipped on pine needles and slid down the slope into Miss Mackenzie's nasturtium bed. Finding no escape, he gave a bright smile and said, 'Good morning, Miss.'

'Good morning,' said Miss Mackenzie severely. 'Would you mind moving out of my flower bed?'

The boy stepped gingerly over the nasturtiums, and looked at Miss Mackenzie with appealing eyes.

'You ought to be in school,' she said. 'What are you doing here?' 'Picking flowers, Miss.' He held up a bunch of ferns and wild flowers.
'Oh,' Miss Mackenzie was disarmed. It had been a long time since she had seen a boy taking an interest in flowers.
'Do you like flowers?' she asked.

'Yes, Miss. I'm going to be a botan...a botanitist.'

'You mean a botanist?'

'Yes, Miss.'

'That's unusual. Do you know the names of these flowers?'

'This is a buttercup,' he said, showing her a small golden flower. 'But I don't know what this is,' he said, holding out a pale, pink flower with a heart-shaped leaf.

'It's a wild begonia,' said Miss Mackenzie. 'And that purple stuff is salvia. Do you have any books on flowers?'

'No, Miss.'

'Come in and I'll show you one.' She led the boy into a small front room crowded with furniture, books, vases, and jam jars. He sat awkwardly on the edge of the chair. The cat jumped immediately on to his knees and settled down, purring softly.

'What's your name?' asked Miss Mackenzie, as she rummaged through her books.

'Anil, Miss.'

'And where do you live?' 'When school closes, I go to Delhi. My father has a business there.'

'Oh, and what's that?'

'Bulbs, Miss.'

'Flower bulbs?'

'No, electric bulbs.'

'Ah, here we are!' she said taking a heavy tome from the shelf. 'Flora Himaliensis, published in 1892, and probably the only copy in India. This is a valuable book, Anil. No other naturalist has recorded as many wild Himalayan flowers. But there are still many plants unknown to the botanists who spend all their time at microscopes instead of in the mountains. Perhaps you'll do something about that one day.'

'Yes, Miss.'

She lit the stove and put the kettle on for tea. And then the old English lady and the small Indian boy sat side by side, absorbed in the book. Miss Mackenzie pointed out many flowers that grew around the hill-station, while the boy made notes of their names and seasons.

'May I come again?' asked Anil, when finally he rose to go.

'If you like,' said Miss Mackenzie. 'But not during school hours. You mustn't miss your classes.'

After that, Anil visited Miss Mackenzie about once a week, and nearly always brought a wild flower for her to identify. She looked forward to the boy's visits. Sometimes when more than a week passed and he didn't come, she would grumble at the cat.

By the middle of October, with only a fortnight left before school closed, snow fell on the distant mountains. One peak stood high above the others, a white pinnacle againt an azure sky. When the sun set, the peak turned from orange to pink to red.

'How high is that mountain?' asked Anil.

'It must be over 15,000 feet,' said Miss Mackenzie. 'I always wanted to go there, but there is no proper road. On the lower slopes, there'll be flowers that you don't get here: blue gentian, purple columbine.' The day before school closed, Anil came to say goodbye. As he was about to leave, Miss Mackenzie thrust the Flora Himaliensis into his hands. 'It's a gift,' she said.

'But I'll be back next year, and I'll be able to look at it then,' he protested. 'Besides, it's so valuable!'

'That's why I'm giving it to you. Otherwise, it will fall into the hands of the junk dealers.'

'But, Miss…'

'Don't argue.'

The boy tucked the book under his arm, stood at attention, and said, 'Goodbye, Miss Mackenzie.' It was the first time he had spoken her name.

Strong winds soon brought rain and sleet, killing the flowers in the garden. The cat stayed indoors, curled up at the foot of the bed. Miss Mackenzie wrapped herself in old shawls and mufflers, but still felt cold. Her fingers grew so stiff that it took almost an hour to open a can of baked beans. Then it snowed, and for several days the milkman did not come.

Tired, she spent most of her time in bed. It was the warmest place. She kept a hot-water bottle against her back, and the cat kept her feet warm. She dreamed of spring and summer. In three months, the primroses would be out, and Anil would return. One night the hot-water bottle burst, soaking the bed. The sun didn't shine for several days, and the blankets remained damp. Miss Mackenzie caught a chill and had to keep to her cold, uncomfortable bed.

A strong wind sprang up one night and blew the bedroom window open. Miss Mackenzie was too weak to get up and close it. The wind swept the rain and sleet into the room. The cat snuggled close to its mistress's body. Towards morning, the body lost its warmth, and the cat left the bed and started scratching about on the floor.

As sunlight streamed through the window, the milkman arrived. He poured some milk into the saucer on the doorstep, and the cat jumped down from the window-sill.

The milkman called out a greeting to Miss Mackenzie. There was no answer. Knowing she was always up before sunrise, he poked his head in the open window and called again.

Miss Mackenzie did not answer. She had gone to the mountain, where the blue gentian and the purple columbine grow.

Romi and the Wildfire

As Romi was about to mount his bicycle, he saw smoke rising from behind the distant line of trees.

'It looks like a forest fire,' said Prem, his friend and classmate.

'It's well to the east,' said Romi. 'Nowhere near the road.'

'There's a strong wind,' said Prem, looking at the dry leaves swirling across the road.

It was the middle of May, and it hadn't rained in the Terai for several weeks. The grass was brown, the leaves of the trees covered with dust. Even though it was getting on to six o'clock in the evening, the boys' shirts were damp with sweat.

'It will be getting dark soon,' said Prem. 'You'd better spend the night at my house.'

'No, I said I'd be home tonight. My father isn't keeping well. The doctor has given me some tablets for him.'

'You'd better hurry, then. That fire seems to be spreading.'

'Oh, it's far off. It will take me only forty minutes to ride through the forest. 'Bye, Prem – see you tomorrow!'

Romi mounted his bicycle and pedalled off down the main road of the village, scattering stray hens, stray dogs and stray villagers.

'Hey, look where you're going!' shouted an angry villager, leaping out of the way of the oncoming bicycle. 'Do you think you own the road?'

‘Of course I own it,’ called Romi cheerfully, and cycled on.

His own village lay about seven miles distant, on the other side of the forest; but there was only a primary school in his village, and Romi was now in High School. His father, who was a fairly wealthy sugarcane farmer, had only recently bought him the bicycle. Romi didn’t care too much for school and felt there weren’t enough holidays; but he enjoyed the long rides, and he got on well with his classmates.

He might have stayed the night with Prem had it not been for the tablets which the Vaid – the village doctor – had given him for his father.

Romi's father was having back trouble, and the medicine had been specially prepared from local herbs.

Having been given such a fine bicycle, Romi felt that the least he could do in return was to get those tablets to his father as early as possible.

He put his head
down and rode swiftly
out of the village. Ahead of
him, the smoke rose from the burning
forest and the sky glowed red.

He had soon left the village far behind. There was a slight climb, and Romi had to push harder on the pedals to get over the rise. Once over the top, the road went winding down to the edge of the sub-tropical forest.

This was the part Romi enjoyed most. He relaxed, stopped pedalling, and allowed the bicycle to glide gently down the slope. Soon the wind was rushing past him, blowing his hair about his face and making his shirt billow out behind. He burst into song.

A dog from the village ran beside him, barking furiously. Romi shouted to the dog, encouraging him in the race.

Then the road straightened out, and Romi began pedalling again.

The dog, seeing the forest ahead, turned back to the village. It was afraid of the forest.

The smoke was thicker now, and Romi caught the smell of burning timber. But ahead of him the road was clear. He rode on.

It was a rough, dusty road, cut straight through the forest. Tall trees grew on either side, cutting off the last of the daylight. But the spreading glow of the fire on the right lit up the road, and giant tree-shadows danced before the boy on the bicycle.

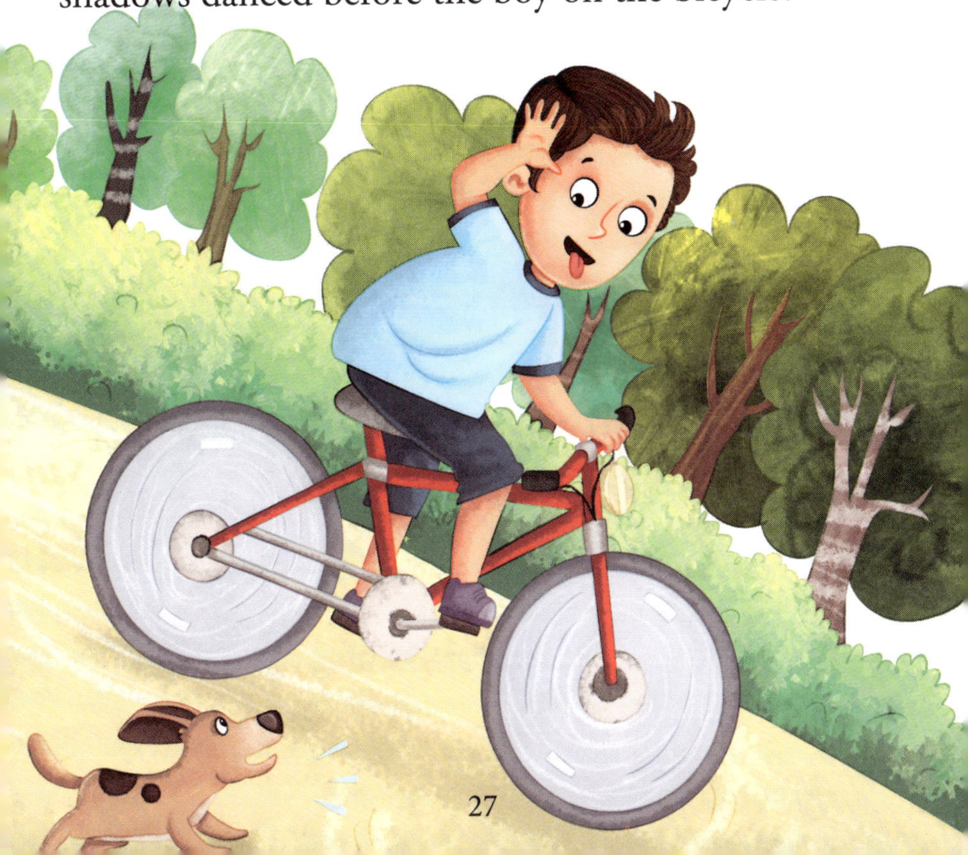

Usually the road was deserted. This evening it was alive with wild creatures fleeing from the forest fire. The first animal that Romi saw was a hare, leaping across the road in front of him. It was followed by several more hares. Then a band of monkeys streamed across, chattering excitedly.

'They'll be safe on the other side,' thought Romi. The fire won't cross the road.

But it was coming closer. And realising this, Romi pedalled harder. In half-an-hour he should be out of the forest.

Suddenly, from the side of the road, several pheasants rose in the air, and with a whoosh, flew low across the path, just in front of the oncoming bicycle. Taken by surprise, Romi fell off. When he picked himself up and began brushing his clothes, he saw that his knee was bleeding. It wasn't a deep cut, but he allowed it to bleed a little, took out his handkerchief and bandaged his knee. Then he mounted the bicycle again.

He rode a bit slower now, because birds and animals kept coming out of the bushes.

Not only pheasants but smaller birds, too, were streaming across the road – parrots, jungle crows, owls, magpies – and the air was filled with their cries.

'Everyone's on the move,' thought Romi. It must be a really big fire.

He could see the flames now, reaching out from behind the trees on his right, and he could hear the crackling as the dry leaves caught fire. The air was hot on his face. Leaves, still alight or turning to cinders, floated past.

A herd of deer crossed the road, and Romi had to stop until they had passed. Then he mounted again and rode on; but now, for the first time, he was feeling afraid.

From ahead came a faint clanging sound. It wasn't an animal's sound, Romi was sure of that. A fire-engine? There were no fire-engines within fifty miles but.

The clanging came nearer, and Romi discovered that the noise came from a small boy who was running along the forest path, two milk-cans clattering at his side 'Teju!' called Romi, recognising the boy from a neighbouring village. 'What are you doing out here?'

'Trying to get home, of course,' said Teju, panting along beside the bicycle.

'Jump on,' said Romi, stopping for him.

Teju was only eight or nine – a couple of years younger than Romi. He had come to deliver milk to some road-workers, but the workers had left at the first signs of the fire, and Teju was hurrying home with his cans still full of milk.

He got up on the cross-bar of the bicycle, and Romi moved on again. He was quite used to carrying friends on the crossbar.

'Keep beating your milk-cans,' said Romi. 'Like that, the animals will know we are coming. My bell doesn't make enough noise. I'm going to get a horn for my cycle!'

'I never knew there were so many animals in the jungle,' said Teju. 'I saw a python in the middle of the road. It stretched right across!'

'What did you do?'

'Just kept running and jumped right over it!'

Teju continued to chatter but Romi's thoughts were on the fire, which was much closer now. Flames shot up from the dry grass and ran up the trunks of trees and along the branches. Smoke billowed out above the forest.

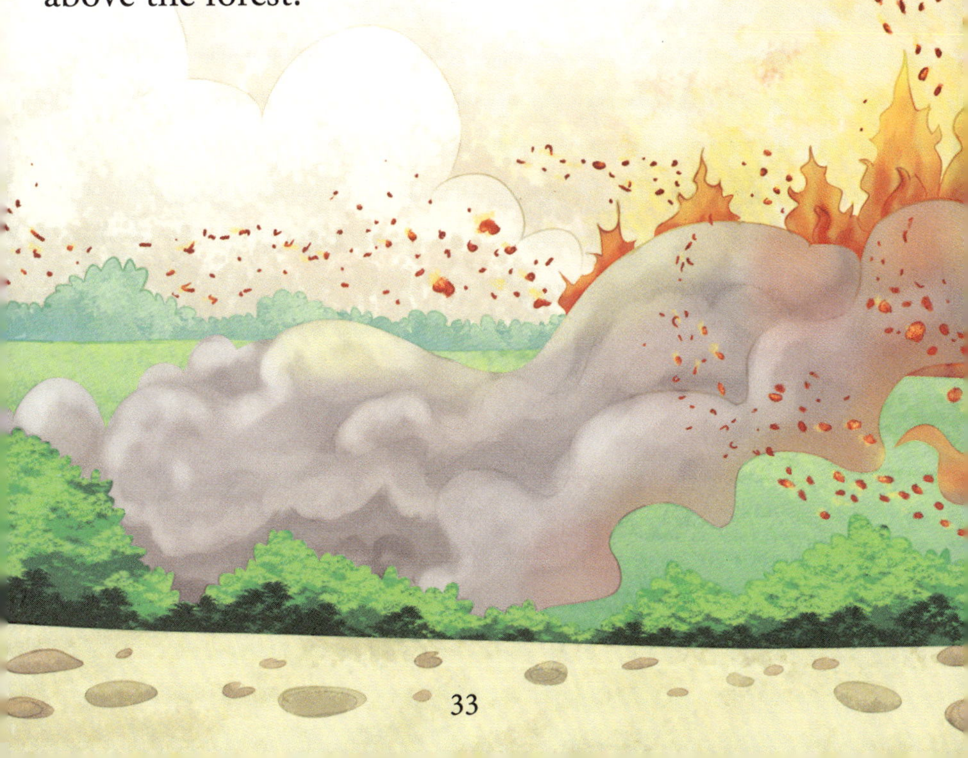

Romi's eyes were smarting and his hair and eyebrows felt scorched. He was feeling tired but he couldn't stop now, he had to get beyond the range of the fire. Another ten or fifteen minutes of steady riding would get them to the small wooden bridge that spanned the little river separating the forest from the sugarcane fields.

Once across the river, they would be safe. The fire could not touch them on the other side, because the forest ended at the river's edge. But could they get to the river in time?

Clang, clang, clang, went Teju's milk-cans. But the sound of the fire grew louder too.

A tall silk-cotton tree, its branches leaning across the road, had caught fire. They were almost beneath it when there was a crash and a burning branch fell to the ground a few yards in front of them.

The boys had to get off the bicycle and leave the road, forcing their way through a tangle of thorny bushes on the left, dragging and pushing at the bicycle and only returning to the road some distance ahead of the burning tree.

‘We won’t get out in time,’ said Teju, back on the cross-bar but feeling disheartened.
‘Yes, we will,’ said Romi, pedalling with all his might. ‘The fire hasn’t crossed the road as yet.’
Even as he spoke, he saw a small flame leap up from the grass on the left. It wouldn’t be long before more sparks and burning leaves were blown across the road to kindle the grass on the other side.

'Oh, look!' exclaimed Romi, bringing the bicycle to a sudden stop.
'What's wrong now?' asked Teju, rubbing his sore eyes. And then, through the smoke, he saw what was stopping them.
An elephant was standing in the middle of the road.
Teju slipped off the cross-bar, his cans rolling on the ground, bursting open and spilling their contents.

The elephant was about forty feet away. It moved about restlessly, its big ears flapping as it turned its head from side to side, wondering which way to go. From far to the left, where the forest was still untouched, a herd of elephants moved towards the river. The leader of the herd raised his trunk and trumpeted a call. Hearing it, the elephant on the road raised its own trunk and trumpeted a reply. Then it shambled off into the forest, in the direction of the herd, leaving the way clear.

'Come, Teju, jump on!' urged Romi. 'We can't stay here much longer!'

Teju forgot about his milk-cans and pulled himself up on the cross-bar. Romi ran forward with the bicycle, to gain speed, and mounted swiftly. He kept as far as possible to the left of the road, trying to ignore the flames, the crackling, the smoke and the scorching heat.

It seemed that all the animals who could get away had done so. The exodus across the road had stopped.

‘We won’t stop again,’ said Romi, gritting his teeth. ‘Not even for an elephant!’

‘We’re nearly there!’ said Teju. He was perking up again.

A jackal, overcome by the heat and smoke, lay in the middle of the path, either dead or unconscious. Romi did not stop. He swerved round the animal. Then he put all his strength into one final effort.

He covered the last hundred yards at top speed, and then they were out of the forest, free-wheeling down the sloping road to the river.

'Look!' shouted Teju. 'The bridge is on fire!'

Burning embers had floated down onto the small wooden bridge, and the dry, ancient timber had quickly caught fire. It was now burning fiercely.

Romi did not hesitate. He left the road, riding the bicycle over sand and pebbles. Then with a rush they went down the river-bank and into the water.

The next thing they knew they were splashing around, trying to find each other in the darkness.
'Help!' cried Teju. 'I'm drowning!'
'Don't be silly,' said Romi. 'The water isn't deep – it's only up to the knees. Come here and grab hold of me.'
Teju splashed across and grabbed Romi by the belt.
'The water's so cold,' he said, his teeth chattering.
'Do you want to go back and warm yourself?' asked Romi. 'Some people are never satisfied. Come on, help me get the bicycle up. It's down here, just where we are standing.'

Together they managed to heave the bicycle out of the water and stand it upright.

'Now sit on it,' said Romi. 'I'll push you across.'

'We'll be swept away,' said Teju.

'No, we won't. There's not much water in the river at this time of the year. But the current is quite strong in the middle, so sit still. All right?'

'All right,' said Teju nervously.

Romi began guiding the bicycle across the river, one hand on the seat and one hand on the handlebar. The river was shallow and sluggish in midsummer; even so, it was quite swift in the middle. But having got safely out of the burning forest, Romi was in no mood to let a little river defeat him.

He kicked off his shoes, knowing they would be lost; and then gripping the

smooth stones of the riverbed with his toes, he concentrated on keeping his balance and getting the bicycle and Teju through the middle of the stream. The water here came up to his waist, and the current would have been too strong for Teju. But when they reached the shallows, Teju got down and helped Romi push the bicycle.

They reached the opposite bank, and sank down on the grass.

'We can rest now,' said Romi. 'But not all night – I've got some medicine to give to my father.' He felt in his pockets and found that the tablets in their envelope, had turned into a soggy mess. 'Oh well, he had to take them with water anyway,' he said.

They watched the fire as it continued to spread through the forest. It had crossed the road down by which they had come. The sky was a bright red, and the river reflected the colour of the sky.

Several elephants had found their way down to the river. They were cooling off by spraying water on each other with their trunks. Further downstream there were deer and other animals.

Romi and Teju looked at each other in the glow from the fire. They hadn't known each other very well before. But now they felt they had been friends for years.

'What are you thinking about?' asked Teju.
'I'm thinking,' said Romi, 'that even if the fire is out in a day or two, it will be a long time before the bridge is repaired. So it will be a nice long holiday from school!'
'But you can walk across the river,' said Teju. 'You just did it.'
'Impossible,' said Romi. 'It's much too swift.'

The Kitemaker

There was but one tree in the street known as Gali Ram Nath—an ancient banyan that had grown through the cracks of an abandoned mosque—and little Ali's kite was caught in its branches. The boy, barefoot and clad only in a torn shirt, ran along the cobbled stones of the narrow street to where his grandfather sat nodding dreamily in the sunshine in their back courtyard.

'Grandfather!' shouted the boy. 'My kite has gone!'

The old man woke from his daydream with a start and, raising his head, displayed a beard that would have been white had it not been dyed red with mehendi leaves. 'Did the twine break?' he asked. 'I know that kite twine is not what it used to be.'

'No, Grandfather, the kite is stuck in the banyan tree.' The old man chuckled. 'You have yet to learn how to fly a kite properly, my child. And I am too old to teach you, that's the pity of it.

But you shall have another.'

He had just finished making a new kite from bamboo, paper and thin silk, and it lay in the sun, firming up. It was a pale pink kite, with a small green tail. The old man handed it to Ali, and the boy raised himself on his toes and kissed his grandfather's hollowed-out cheek.

'I will not lose this one,' he said. 'This kite will fly like a bird.'

And he turned on his heels and skipped out of the courtyard. The old man remained dreaming in the sun. His kite shop was gone, the premises long since sold to a junk dealer; but he still made kites, for his own amusement and for the benefit of his grandson, Ali. Not many people bought kites these days.

Adults disdained them, and children preferred to spend their money at the cinema. Moreover, there were not many open spaces left for the flying of kites. The city had swallowed up the open grassland that had stretched from the Old

Fort's walls to the river bank.

But the old man remembered a time when grown men flew kites, and great battles were fought, the kites swerving and swooping in the sky, tangling with each other until the string of one was severed. Then the defeated but liberated kite would float away into the blue unknown. There was a good deal of betting, and money frequently changed hands. Kite-flying was then the sport of kings, and the old man remembered how the nawab himself would come down to the riverside with his retinue to participate in this noble pastime.

There was time, then, to spend an idle hour with a gay, dancing strip of paper. Now everyone hurried, in a heat of hope, and delicate things like kites and daydreams were trampled underfoot. He, Mehmood the kitemaker, had in the prime of his life been well-known throughout the city. Some of his more elaborate kites once sold for as much as three or four rupees each.

At the request of the nawab he had once made a very special kind of kite, unlike any that had been seen in the district. It consisted of a series of small, very light paper disks trailing on a thin bamboo frame.

To the end of each disk he fixed a sprig of grass, forming a balance on both sides. The surface of the foremost disk was slightly convex, and a fantastic face was painted on it, having two eyes made of small mirrors. The disks, decreasing in size from head to tail, assumed an undulatory form and gave the kite the appearance of a crawling serpent. It required great skill to raise this cumbersome device from the ground, and only Mehmood could manage it.

Everyone had heard of the 'Dragon Kite' that Mehmood had built, and word went round that it possessed supernatural powers. A large crowd assembled in the open to watch its first public launching in the presence of the nawab. At the first attempt it refused to leave the ground. The disks made a plaintive, protesting sound, and the sun was trapped in the little mirrors, making the kite a living, complaining creature.

Then the wind came from the right direction, and the Dragon Kite soared into the sky, wriggling its way higher and higher, the sun still glinting in its devil eyes.

And when it went very high, it pulled fiercely at the twine, and Mehmood's young sons had to help him with the reel. Still the kite pulled, determined to be free, to break loose, to live a life of its own. And eventually it did so.

The twine snapped, the kite leapt away towards the sun, sailing heavenward until it was lost to view. It was never found again, and Mehmood wondered afterwards if he had made too vivid, too living a thing of the great kite. He did not make another like it. Instead he presented to the nawab a musical kite: one that made a sound like a violin when it rose into the air.

Those were more leisurely, more spacious days. But the nawab had died years ago, and his descendants were almost as poor as Mehmood himself.

Kitemakers, like poets, once had their patrons; but now no one knew Mehmood, simply because there were too many people in the gali, and they could not be bothered with their neighbours. When Mehmood was younger and had fallen sick, everyone in the neighbourhood had come to ask after his health; but now, when his days were drawing to a close, no one visited him. Most of his old friends were dead and his sons had grown up: one was working in a local garage and the other, who was in Pakistan at the time of the Partition, had not been able to rejoin his relatives.

The children who had bought kites from him ten years ago were now grown men, struggling for a living; they did not have time for the old man and his memories. They had grown up in a swiftly changing and competitive world, and they looked at the old kitemaker and the banyan tree with the same indifference. Both were taken for granted—permanent fixtures that were of no concern to the raucous, sweating mass of humanity that surrounded them. No longer did people gather under the banyan tree to discuss their problems and their plans; only in the summer months did a few seek shelter from the fierce sun.

But there was the boy, his grandson. It was good that Mehmood's son worked close by, for it gladdened the old man's heart to watch the small boy at play in the winter sunshine, growing under his eyes like a young and well-nourished sapling putting forth new leaves each day. There is a great affinity between trees and men.

We grow at much the same pace, if we are not hurt or starved or cut down. In our youth we are resplendent creatures, and in our declining years we stoop a little, we remember, we stretch our brittle limbs in the sun, and then, with a sigh, we shed our last leaves.

Mehmood was like the banyan, his hands gnarled and twisted like the roots of the ancient tree. Ali was like the young mimosa planted at the end of the courtyard. In two years, both he and the tree would acquire the strength and confidence of their early youth.

The voices in the street grew fainter, and Mehmood
wondered if he was going to fall asleep and dream, as he so often did, of a kite so beautiful and powerful that it would resemble the great white bird of the Hindus—Garuda, Lord Vishnu's famous steed. He would like to make a wonderful new kite for little Ali. He had nothing else to leave the boy.

He heard Ali's voice in the distance, but did not realise that the boy was calling him. The voice seemed to come from very far away.

Ali was at the courtyard door, asking if his mother had as yet returned from the bazaar. When Mehmood did not answer, the boy came forward repeating his question. The sunlight was slanting across the old man's head, and a small white butterfly rested on his flowing beard. Mehmood was silent; and when Ali put his small brown hand on the old man's shoulder, he met with no response. The boy heard a faint sound, like the rubbing of marbles in his pocket.

Suddenly afraid, Ali turned and moved to the door, and then ran down the street shouting for his mother. The butterfly left the old man's beard and flew to the mimosa tree, and a sudden gust of wind caught the torn kite and lifted it in the air, carrying it far above the struggling city into the blind blue sky.

RUSKIN BOND

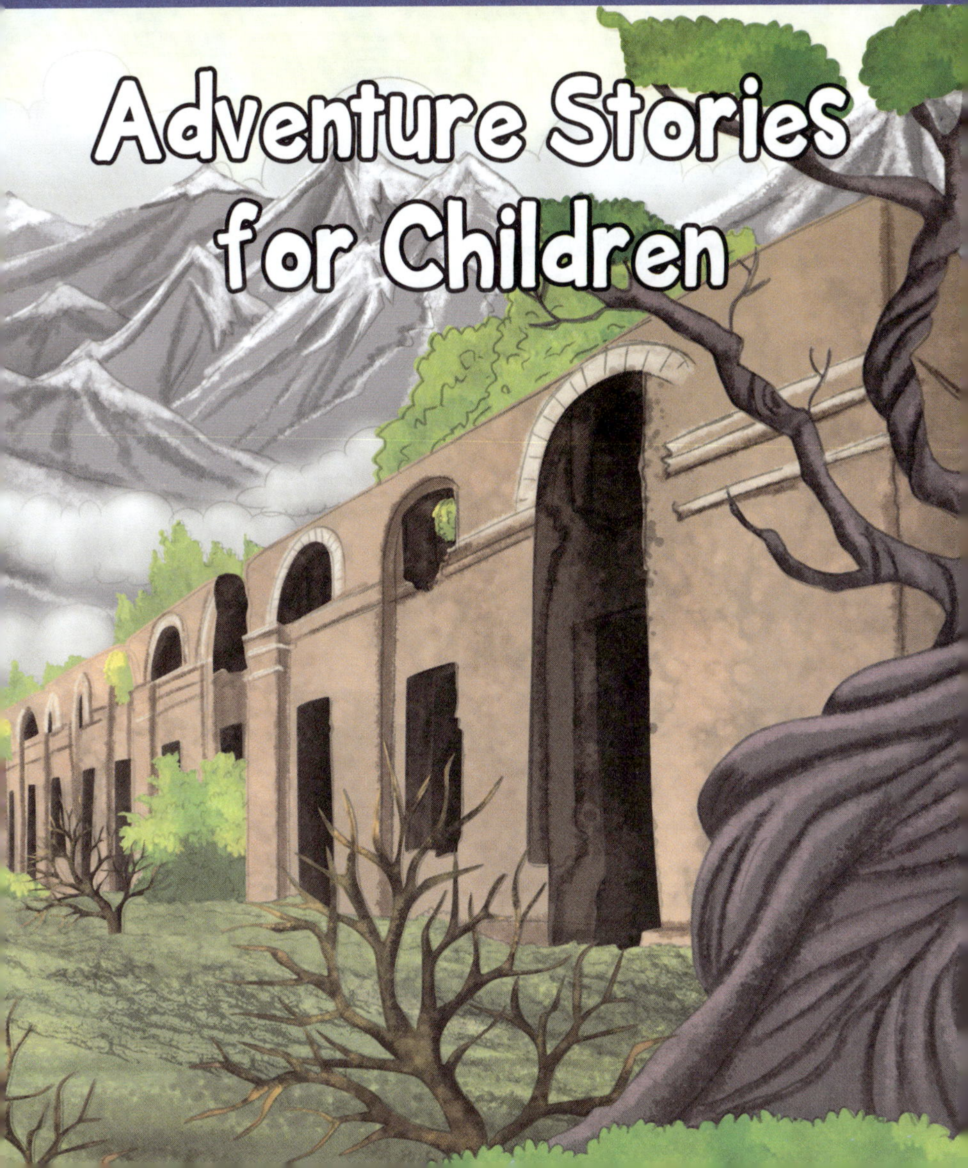

B. Jain Publishers (P) Ltd.

D-157, Sector 63, Noida - 201307, U.P

Registered office: 1921/10, Chuna Mandi, Paharganj, New Delhi-110055

Published in arrangement with Rupa Publications India (P) Ltd.

Printed in India

The Zigzag Walk

Uncle Ken always maintained that the best way to succeed in life was to zigzag. 'If you keep going off in new directions,' he declared, 'you will meet new career opportunities!'

Well, opportunities certainly came Uncle Ken's way, but he was not a success in the sense that Dale Carnegie or Deepak Chopra would have defined a successful man…

In a long life devoted to 'muddling through' with the help of the family, Uncle Ken's many projects had included a chicken farm (rather like the one operated by Ukridge in Wodehouse's Love Among the Chickens) and a mineral water bottling project. For this latter enterprise, he bought a thousand old soda-water bottles and filled them with sulphur water from the springs, five miles from Dehra.

It was good stuff, taken in small quantities, but drunk one bottle at a time it proved corrosive—'sulphur and brimstone' as one irate customer described it—and angry buyers demonstrated in front of the house, throwing empty bottles over the wall into grandmother's garden.

Grandmother was furious—more with Uncle Ken than with the demonstrators—and made him give everyone's money back.

'You have to be healthy and strong to take sulphur water,' he explained later.

'I thought it was supposed to make you healthy and strong,' I said.

Grandfather remarked that it did not compare with plain soda-water, which he took with his whisky. 'Why don't you just bottle soda-water?' he said, 'there's a much bigger demand for it.'

But Uncle Ken believed that he had to be original in all things.

'The secret to success is to zigzag,' he said.
'You certainly zigzagged round the garden when your customers were throwing their bottles back at you,' said Grandmother.
Uncle Ken also invented the zigzag walk.

The only way you could really come to know a place well, was to walk in a truly haphazard way. To make a zigzag walk you take the first turning to the left, the first to the right, then the first to the left and so on. It can be quite fascinating provided you are in no hurry to reach your destination. The trouble was that Uncle Ken used this zigzag method even when he had a train to catch.

When Grandmother asked him to go to the station to meet Aunt Mabel and her children, who were arriving from Lucknow, he zigzagged through the town, taking in the botanical gardens in the west and the limestone factories to the east, finally reaching the station by way of the goods yard, in order as he said, 'to take them by surprise'.

Nobody was surprised, least of all Aunt Mabel who had taken a tonga and reached the house while Uncle Ken was still sitting on the station platform, waiting for the next train to come in. I was sent to fetch him.

'Let's zigzag home again,' he said.

'Only on one condition, we eat chaat every fifteen minutes,' I said.

So we went home by way of all the most winding bazaars, and in North Indian towns they do tend to zigzag, stopping at numerous chaat and halwai shops, until Uncle Ken had finished his money.

We got home very late and were scolded by everyone; but as Uncle Ken told me, we were pioneers and had to expect to be misunderstood and even maligned. Posterity would recognize the true value of zigzagging. 'The zigzag way,' he said, 'is the diagonal between heart and reason.'

In our more troubled times, had he taken to preaching on the subject, he might have acquired a large following of dropouts. But Uncle Ken was the original dropout. He would not have tolerated others.

Had he been a space traveller, he would have gone from star to star, zigzagging across the Milky Way. Uncle Ken would not have succeeded in getting anywhere very fast, but I think he did succeed in getting at least one convert (myself) to see his point: 'When you zigzag, you are not choosing what to see in this world but you are giving the world a chance to see you!'

The Wind on Haunted Hill

Whoo, whoo, whoo, cried the wind as it swept down from the Himalayan snows. It hurried over the hills and passed and hummed and moaned through the tall pines and deodars. There was little on Haunted Hill to stop the wind – only a few stunted trees and bushes and the ruins of a small settlement.

On the slopes of the next hill was a village. People kept large stones on their tin roofs to prevent them from being blown off. There was nearly always a strong wind in these parts. Three children were spreading clothes out to dry on a low stone wall, putting a stone on each piece.

Eleven-year-old Usha, dark-haired and rose-cheeked, struggled with her grandfather's long, loose shirt. Her younger brother, Suresh, was doing his best to hold down a bedsheet, while Usha's friend, Binya, a slightly older girl, helped.

Once everything was firmly held down by stones, they climbed up on the flat rocks and sat there sunbathing and staring across the fields at the ruins on Haunted Hill.

'I must go to the bazaar today,' said Usha.

'I wish I could come too,' said Binya. 'But I have to help with the cows.'

'I can come!' said eight-year-old Suresh. He was always ready to visit the bazaar, which was three miles away, on the other side of the hill.

'No, you can't,' said Usha. 'You must help Grandfather chop wood.'

'Won't you feel scared returning alone?' he asked. 'There are ghosts on Haunted Hill!'

'I'll be back before dark. Ghosts don't appear during the day.' 'Are there lots of ghosts in the ruins?' asked Binya. 'Grandfather says so. He says that over a hundred years ago, some Britishers lived on the hill. But the settlement was always being struck by lightning, so they moved away.'

'But if they left, why is the place visited by ghosts?'
'Because – Grandfather says – during a terrible storm, one of the houses was hit by lightning, and everyone in it was killed. Even the children.'
'How many children?'

'Two. A boy and his sister. Grandfather saw them playing there in the moonlight.'

'Wasn't he frightened?'

'No. Old people don't mind ghosts.'

Usha set out for the bazaar at two in the afternoon. It was about an hour's walk.

The path went through yellow fields of flowering mustard, then along the saddle of the hill, and up, straight through the ruins. Usha had often gone that way to shop at the bazaar or to see her aunt, who lived in the town nearby.

Wild flowers bloomed on the crumbling walls of the ruins, and a wild plum tree grew straight out of the floor of what had once been a hall. It was covered with soft, white blossoms. Lizards scuttled over the stones, while a whistling thrush, its deep purple plumage glistening in the sunshine, sat on a window-sill and sang its heart out.

Usha sang too, as she skipped lightly along the path, which dipped steeply down to the valley and led to the little town with its quaint bazaar.

Moving leisurely, Usha bought spices, sugar and matches. With the two rupees she had saved from her pocket-money, she chose a necklace of amber-coloured beads for herself and some marbles for Suresh. Then she had her mother's slippers repaired at a cobbler's shop.

Finally, Usha went to visit Aunt Lakshmi at her flat above the shops. They were talking and drinking cups of hot, sweet tea when Usha realised that dark clouds had gathered over the mountains. She quickly picked up her things, said goodbye to her aunt, and set out for the village.

Strangely, the wind had dropped. The trees were still, the crickets silent. The crows flew round in circles, then settled on an oak tree.

'I must get home before dark,' thought Usha, hurrying along the path.

But the sky had darkened and a deep rumble echoed over the hills. Usha felt the first heavy drop of rain hit her cheek. Holding the shopping bag close to her body, she quickened her pace until she was almost running. The raindrops were coming down faster now – cold, stinging pellets of rain.

A flash of lightning sharply outlined the ruins on the hill, and then all was dark again. Night had fallen.

'I'll have to shelter in the ruins,' Usha thought and began to run. Suddenly the wind sprang up again, but she did not have to fight it. It was behind her now, helping her along, up the steep path and on to the brow of the hill.

There was another flash of lightning, followed by a peal of thunder. The ruins loomed before her, grim and forbidding.

Usha remembered part of an old roof that would give some shelter. It would be better than trying to go on. In the dark, with the howling wind, she might stray off the path and fall over the edge of the cliff.

Whoo, whoo, whoo, howled the wind. Usha saw the wild plum tree swaying, its foliage thrashing against the ground. She found her way into the ruins, helped by the constant flicker of lightning. Usha placed her hands flat against a stone wall and moved sideways, hoping to reach the sheltered corner. Suddenly, her hand touched something soft and furry, and she gave a startled cry.

Her cry was answered by another – half snarl, half screech – as something leapt away in the darkness. With a sigh of relief Usha realised that it was the cat that lived in the ruins. For a moment she had been frightened, but now she moved quickly along the wall until she heard the rain drumming on a remnant of a tin roof.

Crouched in a corner, she found some shelter. But the tin sheet groaned and clattered as if it would sail away any moment.

Usha remembered that across this empty room stood an old fireplace. Perhaps it would be drier there under the blocked chimney. But she would not attempt to find it just now – she might lose her way altogether.

Her clothes were soaked and water streamed down from her hair, forming a puddle at her feet. She thought she heard a faint cry – the cat again, or an owl? Then the storm blotted out all other sounds.

There had been no time to think of ghosts, but now that she was settled in one place, Usha remembered Grandfather's story about the lightning-blasted ruins. She hoped and prayed that lightning would not strike her.

Thunder boomed over the hills, and the lightning came quicker now. Then there was a bigger flash, and for a moment the entire ruin was lit up.

A streak of blue sizzled along the floor of the building. Usha was staring straight ahead, and, as the opposite wall lit up, she saw, crouching in front of the unused fireplace, two small figures – children! The ghostly figures seemed to look up and stare back at Usha. And then everything was dark again. Usha's heart was in her mouth.

She had seen without doubt, two ghosts on the other side of the room. She wasn't going to remain in the ruins one minute longer.

She ran towards the big gap in the wall through which she had entered. She was halfway across the open space when something – someone – fell against her. Usha stumbled, got up, and again bumped into something. She gave a frightened scream.

Someone else screamed. And then there was a shout, a boy's shout, and Usha instantly recognised the voice.

'Suresh!'

'Usha!'

'Binya!'

They fell into each other's arms, so surprised and relieved that all they could do was laugh and giggle and repeat each other's names.

Then Usha said, 'I thought you were ghosts.'

'We thought you were a ghost,' said Suresh.

'Come back under the roof,' said Usha.

They huddled together in the corner, chattering with excitement and relief.

'When it grew dark, we came looking for you,' said Binya. 'And then the storm broke.'
'Shall we run back together?' asked Usha. 'I don't want to stay here any longer.'
'We'll have to wait,' said Binya. 'The path has fallen away at one place. It won't be safe in the dark, in all this rain.'
'We'll have to wait till morning,' said Suresh, 'and I'm so hungry!'
The storm continued, but they were not afraid now. They gave each other warmth and confidence. Even the ruins did not seem so forbidding.

After an hour the rain stopped, and the thunder grew more distant. Towards dawn the whistling thrush began to sing. Its sweet, broken notes flooded the ruins with music.

As the sky grew lighter, they saw that the plum tree stood upright again, though it had lost all its blossoms.

'Let's go,' said Usha.

Outside the ruins, walking along the brow of the hill, they watched the sky grow pink. When they were some distance away, Usha looked back and said, 'Can you see something behind the wall? It's like a hand waving.'

'It's just the top of the plum tree,' said Binya.
'Goodbye, goodbye…' They heard voices.
'Who said "goodbye"?' asked Usha.
'Not I,' said Suresh.
'Nor I,' said Binya.
'I heard someone calling,' said Usha.
'It's only the wind,' assured Binya.
Usha looked back at the ruins. The sun had come up and was touching the top of the wall.

'Come on,' said Suresh. 'I'm hungry.'
They hurried along the path to the village.
'Goodbye, goodbye…' Usha heard them calling.
Or was it just the wind?

Wild Fruit

It was a long walk to school. Down the hill, through the rhododendron trees, across a small stream, around a bare, brown hill, and then through the narrow little bazaar, past fruit stalls piled high with oranges, guavas, bananas, and apples.

The boy's gaze often lingered on those heaps of golden oranges – oranges grown in the plains, now challenging the pale winter sunshine in the hills. His nose twitched at the sharp smell of melons in summer; his fingers would sometimes touch for a moment the soft down on the skin of a peach. But these were forbidden fruit. The boy hadn't the money for them.

He took one meal at seven in the morning when he left home; another at seven in the evening when he returned from school. There were times – especially when he was at school, and his teacher droned on and on, lecturing on honesty, courage, duty, and self-sacrifice – when he felt very hungry; but on the way to school, or on the way home, there was nearly always the prospect of some wild fruit.

The boy's name was Vijay, and he belonged to a village near Mussoorie. His parents tilled a few narrow terraces on the hill slopes. They grew potatoes, onions, barley, maize; barely enough to feed themselves. When greens were scarce, they boiled the tops of the stinging-nettle and made them into a dish resembling spinach.

Vijay's parents realised the importance of sending him to school, and it didn't cost them much, except for the books. But it was all of four miles to the town, and a long walk makes a boy hungry. But there was nearly always the wild fruit.

The purple berries of the thorny bilberry bushes, ripening in May and June. Wild strawberries, growing in shady places like spots of blood on the deep green monsoon grass. Small, sour cherries, and tough medlars.

Vijay's strong teeth and probing tongue extracted whatever tang or sweetness lay hidden in them. And in March there were the rhododendron flowers. His mother made them into jam. But Vijay liked them as they were.

He placed the petals on his tongue and chewed them till the sweet juice trickled down his throat. But in November, there was no wild fruit. Only acorns on the oak trees, and they were bitter, fit only for the monkeys.

He walked confidently through the bazaar, strong in the legs. He looked a healthy boy, until you came up close and saw the patches on his skin and the dullness in his eyes.

He passed the fruit stalls, wondering who ate all that fruit, and what happened to the fruit that went bad; he passed the sweet shop, where hot, newly-fried jelabies lay protected like twisted orange jewels in a glass case, and where a fat, oily man raised a knife and plunged it deep into a thick slab of rich amber-coloured halwa.

The saliva built up in Vijay's mouth; there was a dull ache in his stomach. But his eyes gave away nothing of the sharp pangs he felt.

And now, a confectioner's shop.

Glass jars filled with chocolates, peppermints, toffees – sweets he didn't know the names of, English sweets – wrapped in bits of coloured paper.
A boy had just bought a bag of sweets. He had one in his mouth. He was a well-dressed boy; coins jingled in his pocket.

The sweet moved from one cheek to the other. He bit deep into it, and Vijay heard the crunch and looked up. The boy smiled at Vijay, but moved away.

They met again, further along the road. Once again the boy smiled, even looked as though he was about to offer Vijay a sweet; but this time, Vijay shyly looked away.

He did not want it to appear that he had noticed the sweets, or that he hungered for one.
But he kept meeting the boy, who always managed to reappear at some corner, sucking a sweet, moving it about in his mouth, letting it show between his wet lips – a sticky green thing, temptingly, lusciously beautiful.

The bag of sweets was nearly empty.
Reluctantly, Vijay decided that he must overtake the boy, forget all about the sweets, and hurry home. Otherwise, he would be tempted to grab the bag and run!
And then, he saw the boy leave the bag on a bench, look at him once, and smile – smile shyly and invitingly – before moving away.

Was the bag empty? Vijay wondered with mounting excitement. It couldn't be, or it would have blown away almost immediately. Obviously, there were still a few sweets in it. The boy had disappeared. He had gone for his tea, and Vijay could have the rest of the sweets. Vijay took the bag and jammed it into a pocket of his shirt. Then he hurried homewards.

It was getting late, and he wanted to be home before dark.

As soon as he was out of the town, he opened the bag and shook the sweets out. Their red wrappers glowed like rubies in the palm of his hand.

Carefully, he undid a wrapper.

There was no sweet inside, only a smooth, round stone.

Vijay found stones in all the wrappers. In his mind's eye, Vijay saw the smiling face of the boy in the bazaar: a boy who smiled sweetly but exchanged stones for sweets.

Forcing back angry tears, Vijay flung the stones down the hillside. Then he shouldered his bag of books and began the long walk home.

There were patches of snow on the ground. The grass was a dirty brown, the bushes were bare. There is no wild fruit in November.

The Tunnel

It was almost noon, and the jungle was very still, very silent. Heat waves shimmered along the railway embankment where it cut a path through the tall evergreen trees. The railway lines were two straight black serpents disappearing into the tunnel in the hillside.

Suraj stood near the cutting, waiting for the midday train. It wasn't a station, and he wasn't catching a train. He was waiting so that he could watch the steam engine come roaring out of the tunnel.

He had cycled out of Dehra and taken the jungle path until he had come to a small village. He had left the cycle there, and walked over a low scrub-covered hill and down to the tunnel exit.

Now he looked up. He had heard, in the distance, the shrill whistle of the engine. He couldn't see anything, because the train was approaching from the other side of the hill; but presently a sound like distant thunder issued from the tunnel, and he knew the train was coming through.

A second or two later, the steam engine shot out of the tunnel, snorting and puffing like some green, black and gold dragon, some beautiful monster out of Suraj's dreams. Showering sparks left and right, it roared a challenge to the jungle.

Instinctively, Suraj stepped back a few paces. Waves of hot steam struck him in the face. Even the trees seemed to flinch from the noise and heat. And then the train had gone, leaving only a plume of smoke to drift lazily over the tall shisham trees.

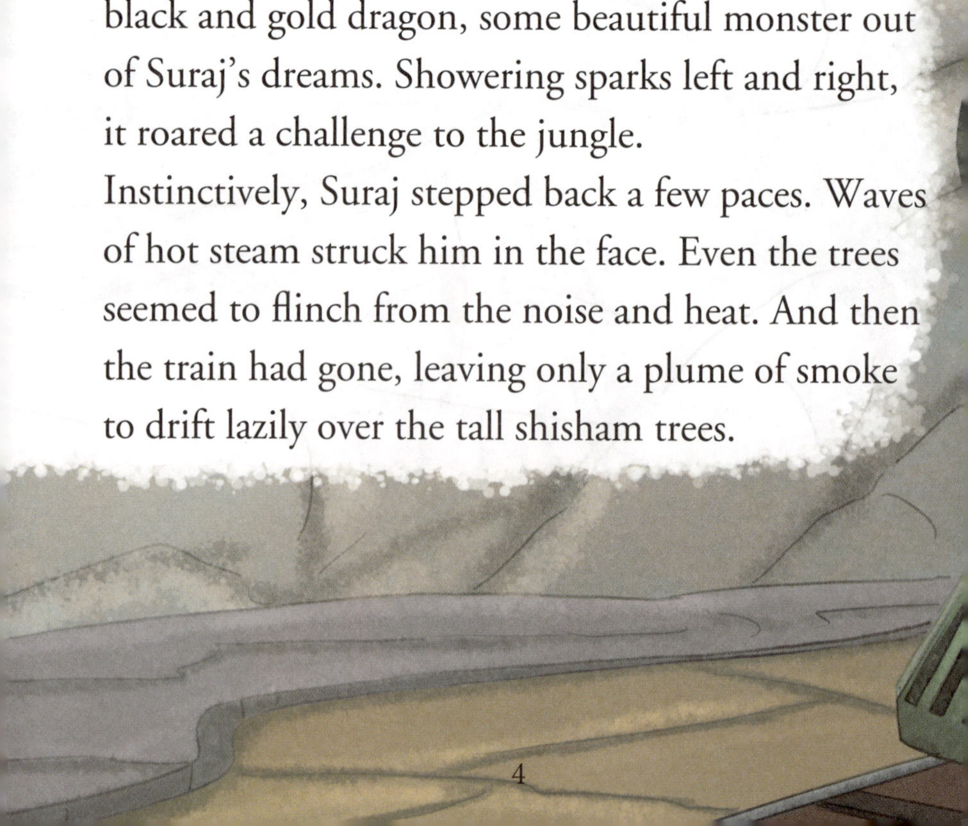

The jungle was still again. No one moved.
Suraj turned from his contemplation of the drifting smoke and began walking along the embankment towards the tunnel.
The tunnel grew darker as he walked further into it. When he had gone about twenty yards it became pitch dark. Suraj had to turn and look back at the opening to reassure himself that there was still daylight outside. Ahead of him, the tunnel's other opening was just a small round circle of light.
The tunnel was still full of smoke from the train, but it would be several hours before another train came through. Till then, the cutting belonged to the jungle again.

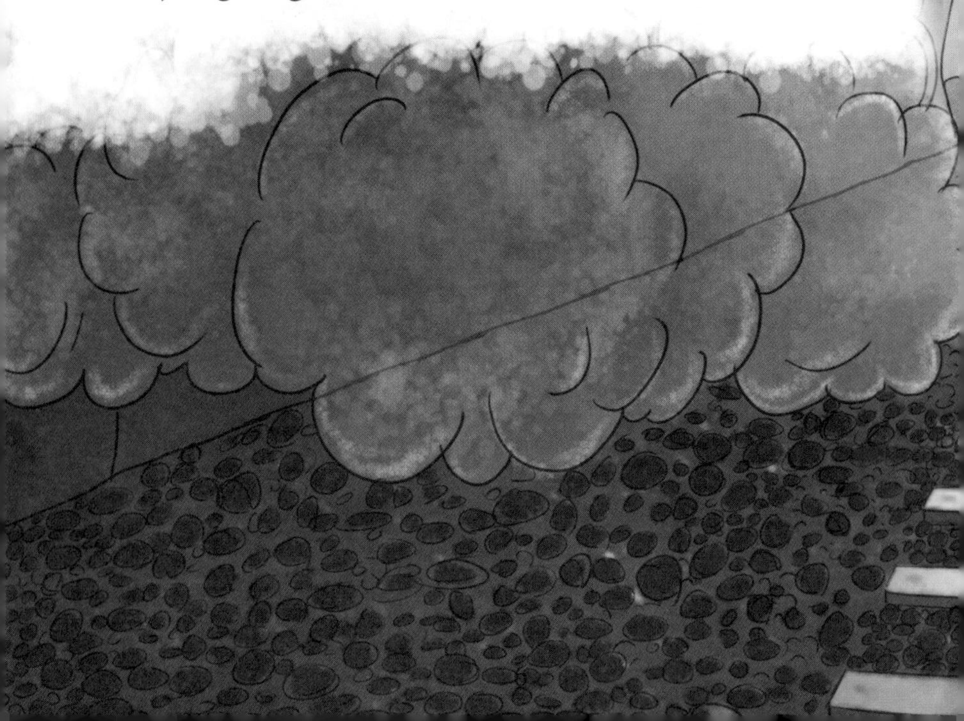

Suraj didn't stop, because there was nothing to do in the tunnel and nothing to see. He had simply wanted to walk through, so that he would know what the inside of a tunnel was really like. The walls were damp and sticky. A bat flew past. A lizard scuttled between the lines.

Coming straight from the darkness into the light, Suraj was dazzled by the sudden glare and put a hand up to shade his eyes. He looked up at the tree-covered hillside and thought he saw something moving between the trees.

It was just a flash of orange and gold, and a long swishing tail. It was there between the trees for a second or two, and then it was gone.

About fifteen metres from the entrance to the tunnel stood the watchman's hut. Marigolds grew in front of the hut, and at the back there was a small vegetable patch.

It was the watchman's duty to inspect the tunnel and keep it clear of obstacles. Every day, before the train came through, he would walk the length of the tunnel. If all was well, he would return to his hut and take a nap.

If something was wrong, he would walk back up the line and wave a red flag and the engine driver would slow down. At night, the watchman lit an oil lamp and made a similar inspection of the tunnel.
Of course, he would not stop the train if there was a porcupine on the line. But if there was any danger to the train, he'd go back up the line and wave his lamp to the approaching engine.

If all was well, he'd hang his lamp at the door of his hut and go to sleep.

He was just settling down on his cot for an afternoon nap when he saw the boy emerge from the tunnel. He waited until Suraj was only a metre or so away and then said: 'Welcome, welcome. I don't often have visitors. Sit down for a while, and tell me why you were inspecting my tunnel.'

'Is it your tunnel?' asked Suraj.

'It is,' said the watchman. 'It is truly my tunnel, since no one else will have anything to do with it. I have only lent it to the Government.'

Suraj sat down on the edge of the cot.

'I wanted to see the train come through,' he said. 'And then, when it had gone, I thought I'd walk through the tunnel.'

'And what did you find in it?'

'Nothing. It was very dark. But when I came out, I thought I saw an animal—up on the hill—but I'm not sure, it moved off very quickly.' 'It was a leopard you saw,' said the watchman. 'My leopard.'

'Do you own a leopard too?'

'I do.'

'And do you lend it to the Government?'

'I do not.'

'Is it dangerous?'

'No, it's a leopard that minds its own business. It comes to this range for a few days every month.'

'Have you been here a long time?' asked Suraj.

'Many years. My name is Sunder Singh.'

'My name's Suraj.'

'There is one train during the day. And there is one train during the night. Have you seen the night mail come through the tunnel?'

'No. At what time does it come?'

'About nine o'clock, if it isn't late. You could come and sit here with me, if you like. And after it has gone, instead of going to sleep I will take you home.'

'I'll ask my parents,' said Suraj. 'Will it be safe?'

'Of course. It is safer in the jungle than in the town. Nothing happens to me out here. But last month, when I went into town, I was almost run over by a bus.'

Sunder Singh yawned and stretched himself out on the cot. 'And now I am going to take a nap, my friend. It is too hot to be up and about in the afternoon.' 'Everyone goes to sleep in the afternoon,' complained Suraj. 'My father lies down as soon as he's had his lunch.' 'Well, the animals also rest in the heat of the day. It is only the tribe of boys who cannot, or will not, rest.'

Sunder Singh placed a large banana leaf over his face to keep away the flies, and was soon snoring gently. Suraj stood up, looking up and down the railway tracks. Then he began walking back to the village.

The following evening, towards dusk, as the flying foxes swooped silently out of the trees, Suraj made his way to the watchman's hut.

It had been a long hot day, but now the earth was cooling, and a light breeze was moving through the trees. It carried with it the scent of mango blossoms, the promise of rain.

Sunder Singh was waiting for Suraj. He had watered his small garden, and the flowers looked cool and fresh. A kettle was boiling on a small oil stove.

'I am making tea,' he said. 'There is nothing like a glass of hot tea while waiting for a train.'

They drank their tea, listening to the sharp notes of the tailorbird and the noisy chatter of the seven sisters.

As the brief twilight faded, most of the birds fell silent. Sunder Singh lit his oil lamp and said it was time for him to inspect the tunnel.

He moved off towards the tunnel, while Suraj sat on the cot, sipping his tea.

In the dark, the trees seemed to move closer to him. And the nightlife of the forest was conveyed on the breeze—the sharp call of a barking deer, the cry of a fox, the quaint tonk-tonk of a nightjar. There were some sounds that Suraj didn't recognize—sounds that came from the trees, creakings and whisperings, as though the trees were coming to life, stretching their limbs in the dark, shifting a little, flexing their fingers.

Sunder Singh stood inside the tunnel, trimming his lamp. The night sounds were familiar to him and he did not give them much thought; but something else—a padded footfall, a rustle of dry leaves—made him stand still for a few seconds, peering into the darkness. Then, humming softly to himself, he returned to where Suraj was waiting. Ten minutes remained for the night mail to arrive.

As Sunder Singh sat down on the cot beside Suraj, a new sound reached both of them quite distinctly—a rhythmic sawing sound, as of someone cutting through the branch of a tree.

'What's that?' whispered Suraj.

'It's the leopard,' said Sunder Singh. 'I think it's in the tunnel.'

'The train will soon be here,' said Suraj.

'Yes, my friend. And if we don't drive the leopard out of the tunnel, it will be run over and killed. I can't let that happen.'

'But won't it attack us if we try to drive it out?' asked Suraj, beginning to share the watchman's concern. 'Not this leopard. It knows me well. We have seen each other many times. It has a weakness for goats and stray dogs, but it will not harm us. Even so, I'll take my axe with me. You stay here, Suraj.'

'No, I'm coming with you. It will be better than sitting here alone in the dark!'

'All right, but stay close behind me. And remember, there is nothing to fear.'

Raising his lamp, Sunder Singh advanced into the tunnel, shouting at the top of his voice to try and scare away the animal. Suraj followed close behind; but he found he was unable to do any shouting. His throat was quite dry.

They had gone about twenty paces into the tunnel when the light from the lamp fell upon the leopard. It was crouching between the tracks, only five metres away from them. It was not a very big leopard, but it looked lithe and sinewy. Baring its teeth and snarling, it went down on its belly, tail twitching. Suraj and Sunder Singh both shouted together. Their voices rang through the tunnel. And the leopard, uncertain as to how many terrifying humans were there in the tunnel with him, turned swiftly and disappeared into the darkness.

To make sure that it had gone, Sunder Singh and Suraj walked the length of the tunnel. When they returned to the entrance, the rails were beginning to hum. They knew the train was coming.

Suraj put his hand to one of the rails and felt its tremor.

He heard the distant rumble of the train. And then the engine came round the bend, hissing at them, scattering sparks into the darkness, defying the jungle as it roared through the steep sides of the cutting. It charged straight at the tunnel, and into it, thundering past Suraj like the beautiful dragon of his dreams.

And when it had gone, the silence returned and the forest seemed to breathe, to live again. Only the rails still trembled with the passing of the train.

They trembled again to the passing of the same train, almost a week later, when Suraj and his father were both travelling in it. Suraj's father was scribbling in a notebook, doing his accounts. Suraj sat at an open window staring out at the darkness. His father was going to Delhi on a business trip and had decided to take the boy along.

('I don't know where he gets to, most of the time,' he'd complained. 'I think it's time he learnt something about my business.')

The night mail rushed through the forest with its hundreds of passengers. The carriage wheels beat out a steady rhythm on the rails. Tiny flickering lights came and went, as they passed small villages on the fringe of the jungle.

Suraj heard the rumble as the train passed over a small bridge. It was too dark to see the hut near the cutting, but he knew they must be approaching the tunnel. He strained his eyes looking out into the night; and then, just as the engine let out a shrill whistle, Suraj saw the lamp.

He couldn't see Sunder Singh, but he saw the lamp, and he knew that his friend was out there.
The train went into the tunnel and out again; it left the jungle behind and thundered across the endless plains.
Suraj stared out at the darkness, thinking of the lonely cutting in the forest and the watchman with the lamp who would always remain a firefly for those travelling thousands as he lit up the darkness for steam engines and leopards.

Gone Fishing

The house was called 'Undercliff', because that's where it stood—under a cliff. The man who went away—the owner of the house was Robert Astley. And the man who stayed behind—the old family retainer—was Prem Bahadur.

Astley had been gone many years. He was still a bachelor in his late thirties when he'd suddenly decided that he wanted adventure, romance, faraway places; and he'd given the keys of the house to Prem Bahadur—who'd served the family for thirty years—and had set off on his travels.

Someone saw him in Sri Lanka. He'd been heard of in Burma, around the ruby mines at Mogok. Then he turned up in Java, seeking a passage through the Sunda Straits. After that the trail petered out. Years passed. The house in the hill station remained empty.

But Prem Bahadur was still there, living in an outhouse. Every day he opened up Undercliff, dusted the furniture in all the rooms, made sure that the bedsheets and pillowcases were clean, and set out Astley's dressing gown and slippers. In the old days, whenever Astley had come home after a journey or a long tramp in the hills, he had liked to bathe and change into his gown and slippers, no matter what the hour. Prem Bahadur still kept them ready. He was convinced that Robert would return one day.

Astley himself had said so.

'Keep everything ready for me, Prem, old chap. I may be back after a year, or two years, or even longer, but I'll be back, I promise you. On the first of every month I want you to go to my lawyer, Mr Kapoor. He'll give you your salary and any money that's needed for the rates and repairs. I want you to keep the house tip-top?'

'Will you bring back a wife, Sahib?'

'Lord, no! Whatever put that idea in your head?'

'I thought, perhaps—because you wanted the house kept ready...'

'Ready for me, Prem. I don't want to come home and find the old place falling down.'

And so Prem had taken care of the house—although there was no news from Astley. What had happened to him? The mystery provided a talking point whenever local people met on the Mall. And in the bazaar the shopkeepers missed Astley because he was a man who spent freely.

His relatives still believed him to be alive. Only a few months back a brother had turned up—a brother who had a farm—in Canada and could not stay in India for long. He had deposited a further sum with the lawyer and told Prem to carry on as before. The salary provided Prem with his few needs. Moreover, he was convinced that Robert would return.

Another man might have neglected the house and grounds, but not Prem Bahadur. He had a genuine regard for the absent owner. Prem was much older—now almost sixty and none too strong, suffering from pleurisy and other chest troubles—but he remembered Robert as both a boy and a young man. They had been together on numerous hunting and fishing trips in the mountains. They had slept out under the stars, bathed in icy mountain streams, and eaten from the same cooking pot.

Once, when crossing a small river, they had been swept downstream by a flash flood, a wall of water that came thundering down the gorges without any warning during the rainy season. Together they had struggled back to safety. Back in the hill station, Astley told everyone that Prem had saved his life; while Prem was equally insistent that he owed his life to Robert.

This year the monsoon had begun early and ended late. It dragged on through most of September, and Prem Bahadur's cough grew worse and his breathing more difficult. He lay on his charpai on the veranda, staring out at the garden, which was beginning to get out of hand, a tangle of dahlias, snake-lilies and convolvulus. The sun finally came out. The wind shifted from the south-west to the north-west, and swept the clouds away.

Prem Bahadur had taken his charpai into the garden, and was lying in the sun, puffing at his small hookah, when he saw Robert Astley at the gate. He tried to get up but his legs would not oblige him. The hookah slipped from his hand. Astley came walking down the garden path and stopped in front of the old retainer, smiling down at him. He did not look a day older than when Prem Bahadur had last seen him.

'So you have come at last,' said Prem.
'I told you I'd return.'

'It has been many years. But you have not changed.'
'Nor have you, old chap.' 'I have grown old and sick and feeble.'
'You'll be fine now. That's why I've come.'
'I'll open the house,' said Prem, and this time he found himself getting up quite easily.
'It isn't necessary' said Astley.
'But all is ready for you.' 'I know. I have heard of how well you have looked after everything. Come then, let's take a last look round. We cannot stay, you know.' Prem was a little mystified but he opened the front door and took Robert through the drawing rooms and up the stairs to the bedroom. Robert saw the dressing gown and the slippers, and he placed his hand gently on the old man's shoulder.

When they returned downstairs and emerged into the sunlight, Prem was surprised to see himself—or rather his skinny body—stretched out on the charpai. The hookah lay on the ground, where it had fallen.

Prem looked at Astley in bewilderment.

'But who is that—lying there?'

'It was you. Only the husk now, the empty shell. This is the real you, standing here beside me.'

'You came for me?'

'I couldn't come until you were ready. As for me, I left my shell a long time ago. But you were determined to hang on, keeping this house together. Are you ready now?'

'And the house?'

'Others will live in it. Nothing is lost for ever, everything begins again. But come, it's time to go fishing...'

Astley took Prem by the arm, and they walked through the dappled sunlight under the deodars and finally left that place for another.

An Island of Trees

Koki and her grandmother were sitting on a string cot in the shade of an old jackfruit tree, and Grandmother was talking about her father and his great love for trees and flowers. Grandmother said, 'I was never able to get over the feeling that plants and trees loved my father with as much tenderness as he loved them.

I was sitting beside him on the verandah steps one morning, when I noticed the tendril of a creeping vine that was trailing near my feet. As we sat there in the soft winter sunshine, I saw the tendril moving very slowly away from me and towards my father. Twenty minutes later it had crossed the verandah steps and was touching my father's feet.

'There is probably a scientific explanation for the plant's behaviour—something to do with light and warmth—but I like to think that it moved simply because it was fond of my father. 'One felt like drawing close to him. Sometimes when I sat alone beneath a tree I would feel a little lonely or lost. But as soon as my father joined me, the garden would become a happy place, the tree itself more friendly.

'Your great-grandfather had served many years in the Indian Forest Service and so it was natural that he should know, understand and like trees.
On his retirement he built this bungalow on the outskirts of the town, planting the trees that you see around it now: limes, mangoes, oranges and guavas; also jacaranda and laburnum and the Persian lilac. In our valley, given the chance, plants and trees grow tall and strong. 'Of course there were other trees here before the house was built, including an old peepul which had forced its way through the walls of an old, abandoned temple, knocking the bricks down with its vigorous growth.

Peepul trees are great show-offs. Even when there is no breeze, their broad-chested, slim-waisted leaves will spin like tops, determined to attract your attention and invite you into the shade.'

'What happened to the temple?' asked Koki.

'Well, my mother wanted the peepul tree cut down, but my father said he would save both the tree and the temple. So he rebuilt the temple around the tree, and there it is, on the other side of the wall. The tree protects the temple, and the temple protects the tree.

People from these parts feel there's a friendly tree spirit dwelling there, and they bring offerings of flowers and leave them at the base of the tree.

'Did you know that I used to climb trees when I was a girl? This jackfruit was my favourite tree, it's quite easy to climb. You climb it too, don't you?

'Another good tree was the banyan behind the house. Its spreading branches, which hung to the ground and took root again, formed a number of twisting passageways. The tree was older than the house, older than my grandparents.

I could hide in its branches, behind a screen of thick green leaves, and spy on the world below. 'Yes, the banyan tree was a world in itself, populated with small animals and large insects. While the leaves were still pink and tender, they would be visited by the delicate map butterfly, who left her eggs to their care. 'The "honey" on the leaves—a sweet, sticky smear—also attracted the little striped squirrels, who soon grew used to having me in the tree. They became quite bold, accepting food from my hand. 'At night the tree was visited by the hawk-cuckoo. Its shrill nagging cry kept us awake on hot summer nights. We call the bird "papiha", which means "rain is coming!" But, Father said that according to Englishmen living in India, it seemed to be shouting up and up the scale: "Oh dear, oh dear! How very hot it's getting! We feel it…we feel it…we feel it!" 'Well, the banyan has long since gone. It came down in a storm, aerial roots and all. Father planted another, but, as you can see, it's still quite a young tree.

The banyan takes a long time to grow.
'Your great-grandfather wasn't content with planting trees just in the garden or near the house. During the monsoons he would walk into the scrubland and beyond the riverbed, armed with cuttings and saplings, and we would plant them out there, hoping to create a forest. But, grazing cattle always finished that off.

"'No one ever goes there,' I said. 'Who will see your forest?' 'We are not planting it for people to see,' said my father. 'We are planting it for the earth—and for the birds and animals who live on it and need more food and shelter.'

'Father told me why mankind, and not only wild creatures, need trees—for keeping the desert away, for attracting rain, for preventing the banks of rivers from being washed away. But everywhere people are cutting down trees without planting new ones.

If this continues, then one day there will be no forests at all and the world will become one great desert!

'The thought of a world without trees became a sort of nightmare for me. It's one reason why I shall never want to live on a treeless moon! I helped my father in his tree-planting with even greater enthusiasm. 'One day the trees will move again,' he said. "They have been standing still for thousands of years, but one day they will move again. There was a time when trees could walk about like people.

Then, along came a terrible demon and cast a spell over them, rooting them to one place. But they are always trying to move—see how they reach out with their arms!' 'On one of our walks along the river bank about a mile up stream from here, we found an island, a small rocky island in the middle of the riverbed. You know what this riverbed is like—dry during summers but flooded during the monsoons. A young tamarind tree was growing in the middle of the island, and my father said, "If a tamarind can grow here, so can other trees."

'As soon as the monsoon arrived—and while the river could still be crossed—we set out with a number of mango, laburnum, hibiscus and coral tree saplings and cuttings, and spent the better part of a day planting them on the little island. We made one
more visit to the island before the monsoon finally set in. Most of the plants looked quite healthy.

'The monsoon season is the best time for rambling about. At every turn there is something new to see.

Out of earth and rock and leafless bough, the magical touch of the monsoon brings forth new life and verdure. You can almost see the broad-leaved vines growing. Plants spring up in the most unlikely places. A peepul took root on the roof, a mango sprouted on the window sill. My father and I did not wait to remove them, but they had to go if the house was to be prevented from falling down!

"'If you two want to live in a tree, that's all right by me,' said my mother.

'But I like having a roof over my head, and I'm not going to have it brought down by a hanging forest. Already I can see roots breaking in through the ceiling!' 'The visiting trees were carefully removed and transplanted in the garden. Whenever we came indoors from our gardening and sat down to a meal, a ladybird or a caterpillar would invariably walk off our sleeves and wander about the kitchen, much to Mother's annoyance. 'There were flowers in the garden too; my mother loved fragrant flowers like roses and sweet peas and jasmine, and yes, the Queen of the Night.

But my father and I found trees more exciting. They kept growing and changing and attracting birds and other visitors. 'The banyan tree really came to life during the monsoon.
The branches were thick with scarlet figs...

We couldn't eat the berries, but the many birds that gathered in the tree—gossipy rosy-pastors, quarrelsome mynas, cheerful bulbuls and coppersmiths, and sometimes a noisy, bullying crow—would feast on them. And when night fell and the birds were resting, the dark flying foxes flapped heavily about the tree, chewing and munching loudly as they clambered over the branches.

'The tree crickets were a band of willing artistes who would start singing at almost any time of the day. At the height of the monsoon, the banyan tree was like an orchestra with the musicians constantly tuning up. A small flute in my hands, I would add my shrill piping to that of the crickets and cicadas. But they must have thought poorly of my piping because whenever I played, the insects fell silent!

'When I grew up, I was married and went to live with your grandfather in Bombay. We were there for many years, and I could only visit my parents here once or twice in all that time.

I had no brothers, so when my parents died they left the house to me. It will be yours one day. Would you rather live here or in that poky little house in the town?' 'Here!' said Koki. 'But only if you are here too, Granny.' 'The trees will be here,' said Granny. 'And what about the island?' asked Koki. 'The trees you planted with your father—are they still there?'

'You can see them for yourself if you feel like a walk.

But I'll tell you what I found when I came to live here again after twenty years or more. I walked out of the old house and took the same path that my father and I used to take during our walks.

'It was February, I remember, and as I looked across the dry riverbed, my eye was immediately caught by the spectacular red plunges of the coral blossom. In contrast with the dry riverbed, the island was a small green paradise. When I walked over to the trees, I noticed that a number of parrots had come to live in them. A small spotted deer scampered away to hide in a thicket. And a wild pheasant challenged me with a mellow "Who-are-you, who-are-you?"

'But the trees seemed to know me. I am sure they whispered among themselves and beckoned me nearer.

'I ran my hands over their barks and it was like touching the hands of old friends. And looking around, I noticed that other small trees and wild plants and grasses had sprung up under the protection of those whom we had planted there.

'The trees had multiplied! The forest was on the move! In one small corner of the world, my father's dream was coming true, and trees were walking again!'